The Power of Self-Discipline:

5-Minute Exercises to Build Self-Control, Good Habits, and Keep Going When You Want to Give Up

By Peter Hollins,
Author and Researcher at
petehollins.com

Table of Contents

Chapter 1. Mind Over Matter

Rosa became *obsessed* with films after watching *Back to the Future* at the age of eight, and subsequently decided she wanted to be a movie director. There hasn't been any other ambition for her ever since. She always kept her goal of directing in mind, even though for the next twenty years, she never made any concrete steps toward it other than to be an avid movie *watcher*.

Her knowledge of arcane movie trivia was second to none. Whatever hours she didn't spend *watching* films she spent on the Internet and in history books *reading* about them. If she could have gone on the trivia television show *Jeopardy*, she would have been a long-running champion. Rosa had read multiple biographies of all of her favorite directors: Spielberg, Kurosawa, Fellini, Miyazaki, and more.

Yet she never translated this research, knowledge, and information into action. She had a fairly expensive video camera that she kept confined to her closet, as well as an archive of film editing software that she had only used a handful of times. They were all too intimidating and confusing. Moreover, what if she discovered that all her knowledge and preparation weren't enough and she was destined to fail at becoming a director? It was easier to take the path of least resistance and remain in inaction. At least learning about Fellini and Miyazaki's favorite films made her feel productive to some degree, even if she was avoiding the elephant in the room.

One day, she discovered an acquaintance of hers had started a YouTube channel that was quickly amassing millions of views. Out of curiosity, she started viewing the videos and was struck by what she saw. *This wasn't art—the shots weren't framed adequately, her focus was wrong, and the narrative structure was reversed!*

None of the viewers seemed to care, however, as the views continued to increase. What's more, the reviews of the videos were all glowing and encouraging. No one cared about the framing or focus. It was impossible for Rosa to ignore the fact that this person had done far more than Rosa and with far less knowledge and expertise. So Rosa made a dramatic decision. *If she can do it, why can't I?*

For four months she was going to make real, concrete strides toward becoming a director—of anything. It was time to buckle down and keep going when all she wanted to do was give up. No more retreating to her comfort zone; she was going to translate her dreams into reality through sheer willpower and self-discipline. She already had the knowledge; it was just time to put it into action.

She first organized her time into two categories: learn and practice.

During learn time, Rosa methodically studied how to write a script, assemble a plot, and what methods renowned directors used to get the shots they wanted. During practice time, she experimented with different shots and angles, wrote a few scenes, and changed perspectives and storylines to see which ones worked the best. No more was she spending hours watching commentary of old movies she'd seen hundreds of times before. And no more was she letting her equipment gather dust in the closet for fear of not being able to use it correctly. For a while, Rosa was brimming with energy and enthusiasm at finally *doing* something about a dream she had held for so long.

The day those four months ended, Rosa set out to make her film. She found a few local actors who were willing to work for pizza. She herself was the camerawoman. Her cousin was her sound person, and her dog was a prop. When she finished, she put it online and it garnered a few hundred views, mostly from family and friends. Rosa wasn't a professional filmmaker, but these were all steps on the journey to seeing her wishes become reality.

She committed herself to completing one short film every month thereafter. She soon grew a reputation for being one of the speediest and most knowledgeable directors in the business. A scant three years later, one of her short films was entered into a film festival competition, something she never even dreamed about when she was just starting out. While she didn't win any prizes, she still gained recognition and began to be able to support herself through her childhood dream of directing.

One day, all at once it seemed, Rosa took a look at the work she had done and felt genuinely good about how far she'd come. She had done it (or rather, she was well on the path to doing it, and keep on doing it!). All the awkward first attempts, early failures and learning curves almost vanished from her memory and she felt proud, accomplished, and confident in her abilities. She wanted to do even more and go even further.

Some might say Rosa was lucky. Perhaps some other movie buff who never quite made the leap from "thinking about it" to actually doing it. That is partially true—but if Rosa had never made the decision to buckle down and do what she had been avoiding for years, she never would have been in the position to *be* lucky.

So what brought Rosa the success she attained as a director?

She realized just in time that she needed to give herself the gift of self-discipline. She knew that whatever she wanted was behind a door that could only be unlocked by it, and no one else could do it for her. Nobody could push her through that door or open it for her. If she did nothing, she would stay on the wrong side of it forever, dreaming and hoping, yet never any closer to what she craved deep down.

She changed her habits, started thinking methodically, and put her ideas into motion. She didn't expect overnight miracles or get discouraged when her first attempts were a little rough. She didn't accept a lifestyle devoid of challenge or pain, and she willed herself to a goal through hardship and struggle. She didn't give up when she wanted to, as she did for years, and put her goals above a sense of temporary discomfort. In a way, she dimply no longer accepted that *not* striving for her goal was an option for her anymore.

Self-discipline, willpower, self-control, "mind over matter"—whatever you want to call it, that was what Rosa summoned, and that's what this book is about. It's the process of going through what we'd rather avoid, in order to reach what makes us happiest.

Even if you don't quite believe it right now, Rosa possessed no extra superpowers that you lack. If it seems difficult, well, it is. But it was no less difficult for Rosa to get over her sense of doubt and disbelief, than it is for you now to imagine that you could succeed at your dreams. What I mean is—if she can do it, then so can you.

On the surface, it's easy to explain: ensuring that we act in accordance with our intentions. It means focusing our intentions and behaviors in one direction to achieve the life we want. It represents the ability to do what we want *no matter what*. We intellectually and logically know that it's the way to what we want. The only way.

So why did Rosa wait years to act? Why is it so hard for many of us?

Self-discipline and matching a thought to an action involves the mind. The second part—

the action—is not a problem because our arms and legs generally do what we tell them to do. They aren't pulled in different directions by stray thoughts. Even if they don't listen to us the first time, we can physically force them into compliance. But the mind—your thoughts, intentions, and expectations—can't be twisted and forced into anything.

Consider that the goal of most meditation and mindfulness practices is to eliminate all mental chatter to focus on a single thought, or to focus on a physical sensation and *no* thought at all. Control and mastery over our minds are a few of the best weapons against stress and anxiety. Arguably, control over the mind and translating that into action is one of life's most elusive achievements.

Quick—*don't think about the purple elephant wearing a tutu*. Did my warning work? Are you now *not* picturing the elephant standing in a meadow with its big floppy ears and a white sheer tutu? Are you successfully *not* imagining its trunk and thick legs? Probably not. And that's why the mind is such a difficult beast to defeat.

Self-discipline is the creation of a clear path between your internal and external realities, *no matter what.*

No matter if there are no immediate rewards; in fact, the rewards are usually so far away that you can't even fathom them at the moment. No matter that sometimes the progress is so gradual that it's difficult for one to gauge any difference, and if they can't see exactly how they're getting better, then they're apt to give up. No matter that other times, the mind is hijacked by emotions, triggers, and otherwise damaging thought patterns.

This is just a small sampling of what we battle on the road from intentions to actions. However well-intentioned you are, your mind just doesn't care. It has to be coaxed, built, and even tricked into compliance, and that's what you'll learn in this book.

Appropriately, this first chapter is about the various obstacles we face in putting a leash on our minds.

5 Mental Hindrances to Self-Discipline

What blocks us from attaining strong self-discipline? An especially illustrative set of obstacles comes from Buddhist philosophy.

When you think of Buddhism, the world discipline is usually not far away. In fact, discipline is right at the core of Buddhist teachings.

Its tenets emphasize maintaining a sense of control over one's mind and body as a means to fulfillment. In fact, it preaches that we are naturally endowed with the ability to do what we want, and feel contentment at all times. However, we give up those feelings of control to someone or something outside of ourselves; we relinquish our own power to an external force that we perceive has more power. We say, "I can't," "I shouldn't," or "I won't," far more often than we should. We say it so much that we believe that fighting against these powers is useless, and thus we lose power over ourselves. In other words, when we tell ourselves we have no discipline, it ends up being true.

Therefore, Buddhism teaches that a lack of personal power is illusory. It can be difficult to take that power back, but this, of course, is one of the first steps to self-discipline—believing that it's possible and within your control.

Part of the process involves knowing exactly how we're being blocked or prohibited from exercising that control. To that end, there are five areas that cover most, if not all, of the sources of our trepidation in taking control of our lives. If you're just starting to figure out where your shortcomings in self-discipline exist, these five areas are helpful to start investigating yourself. If you're a grizzled veteran seeking new methods, these five areas may provide new perspective on familiar issues. Below are the five mental hindrances:

- giving in to the five senses

- animosity and malice

- apathy and laziness

- anxiety and remorse

- hesitation and doubt

Giving in to the five senses. Control over our thoughts is usurped when we are distracted by our physical surroundings. We put too much attention and importance on information from our senses of sight, sound, smell, hearing, and touch—whether it's physical beauty, the smell of freshly baked bread, a great love song, or a horrible scene of violence. We allow these sensations to overwhelm us and replace our conscious thoughts and goals.

Our senses bring us the most immediate understanding of the external world and help us orient and make sense (quite literally!) of ourselves and our place in the word. But we overstate their importance to us and can forget that we are ultimately in control. Our senses gather data from the world, but it is then up to us whether we get distracted by, attached to, or lost in that data, or whether we can maintain a calm, focused awareness of ourselves despite any stimulus, even as transient sensations pass over us.

Many of us only believe in what we can experience with these senses, or we at least allow them to take over our concentration as we seek to gratify ourselves. We forget ourselves. Our attention becomes like a flimsy balloon blown this way or that way by any breeze that comes along. Sensory information by its very nature is instant gratification. But not everything is beneficial or even deserves our attention. We have a choice.

To attain self-discipline, we need to put sensory information in its proper context: allowing ourselves to indulge in and experience those senses fully but also keeping aware that they are temporary, distracting, and ultimately hindrances.

Animosity and malice. Emotions have the ability to completely override our thoughts of self-discipline, and anger is one of the strongest emotions. People are adept at unconsciously ingraining all emotions adjacent to anger, such as resentment, bitterness, and animosity, into their thought patterns. The destructive power of malice isn't just about what other people do to us, either—it can also be directed toward *ourselves* in the acts of guilt or self-loathing. They have the ability to undermine all of our thoughts and render us practically blind in fits of rage.

We obsess over past miscarriages of justice or fairness that hurt us: the ex who broke your heart, the company that fired you for stupid reasons, or the drive-thru restaurant that got your order wrong. These feelings activate our impulse to exact retribution or punish the people or institutions who have "done us wrong." It's draining at best and self-sabotage at worst. When you act to address animosity and malice, you certainly don't address your goals.

Apathy and laziness. The simple act of *doing* is not usually preferable. Being human takes a lot of work. For many, it's easier to allow themselves and their bodies to seek an escape from constant mental and physical activity by shutting down and feeling nothing. Whatever it takes to get along in the world is just too much for them to deal with, and the end product is apathy and sloth. This is a mental hindrance you are probably quite familiar with.

Humans tend to enjoy the path of least resistance and will seek it whenever possible. The problem is when this becomes an instinctual course of action, with a corresponding inability to break out of it when necessary.

Anxiety and remorse. Like anger, anxiety has the ability to completely overpower your more productive thoughts.

The previous three hindrances show how one can be immobilized by inner thoughts—but anxiety causes you to be mentally *overactive* and do *too much.* Anxiety is the fear of a bad or less-than-perfect outcome leading to agitation and worry, making one become overwhelmed with stress, worry, and then finally remorse after the fact. How can you function if you are crippled with fear? It becomes clear that no action at all is far safer. Self-discipline is relegated to a distant priority compared to safety and security.

Hesitation, disbelief, and uncertainty. Why would you engage in self-discipline if you believe it is all for nothing? For somebody who struggles with doubt, low self-esteem, or insecurity, self-questioning can be a debilitating factor that goes well past the point where introspection remains valuable. "I don't know if I can do this," "Am I doing this right?" "What's the point of this, anyway?" "What the heck is this?"—all these questions serve as barriers to disciplined action.

They indirectly call out our reasons for doing anything or raise just enough uncertainty about a given task that you might abandon it without much resistance—the very opposite of what a self-disciplined person does.

Planning and powering past these doubts is a key to restoring self-discipline. Unfortunately, it's not as easy as self-awareness, as you'll learn in the next section. Though you may be able to solve a couple of your mental hindrances through stopping and pausing, you'll need to address some deeper, biological issues as well.

The Brain That Works Against You

Almost nobody will argue against the importance of self-discipline, even if they know they fall short in practicing it on a daily basis.

Anyone with some life experience under their belt knows that they can accomplish more with a healthy sense of constraint and willpower. If they haven't always exhibited self-control themselves, at least they've seen examples of successful people who *have*—and they'll readily admit that such people at least appear to get more done than those without self-control.

Why do we fight against our own self-interests when it comes to instilling discipline into our own lives? Is it just that we don't want to eat our vegetables? Not quite. Unfortunately, a major reason—a more general reason that directly or indirectly causes each of the five mental hindrances—is the brain itself.

The brain is a network. It's fundamentally composed of nerve cells, or neurons. These neurons communicate to each other through chemical reactions—an impulse in one nerve fiber gets activated, then is converted into a chemical that flies across the gap and is received by another nerve fiber. This act, multiplied by about a trillion times a day, basically controls everything we do, say, or think.

That chemical that's flying across the gap is called a neurotransmitter, and different neurotransmitters are responsible for different communications to the brain. It wouldn't be inaccurate to say that our thoughts and reactions are determined by these chemicals. Self-discipline is especially tied to a specific neurotransmitter: dopamine.

Dopamine is one of the agents that work on the brain's pleasure and reward centers. In other words, when we experience pleasure or reward of some type, dopamine is usually at the root of it—the greater the amount of dopamine released, the greater the pleasure we feel. It happens during and after a pleasurable event—you feel it *while* you are eating a dozen donuts and also *after* you finish a great workout at the gym. However, dopamine is also released in *anticipation* of pleasure or reward, which ties it directly to self-discipline.

It *sabotages* it.

The reality of the matter is that we are all dopamine junkies. We want it right now and as soon as possible. Our brains crave it, and it plays a big part in telling us when to act or stop. This trait makes it difficult for us to ignore something that gives us instant dopamine in favor of delayed dopamine, even if it will be substantially greater at a later point. Why go to the gym when you can eat a pie right now, even if you know what's better for you?

Dopamine is what we seek, and this causes us to be ruled by one of the most well-known theories concerning human behavior—the *pleasure principle*. The reason it's so renowned is because it's also the easiest to understand. The pleasure principle was first raised in public consciousness by the father of psychoanalysis, Sigmund Freud, though researchers as far back as Aristotle in ancient Greece noted how easily we could be manipulated by pleasure and pain.

The pleasure principle asserts that the human mind does everything it can to seek out pleasure and avoid pain. It doesn't think; it doesn't analyze; it just acts like a blind animal urgently moving in the direction that it feels more pleasure and less pain. It doesn't have any sense of restraint. It is primal and unfiltered. It doesn't get simpler than that. An apt comparison, in fact, is a drug addict who will stop at nothing to get another taste of narcotics.

There are a few rules that govern the pleasure principle:

Every decision we make is based on gaining pleasure or avoiding pain in some way. You may have heard about the debate that there is no truly altruistic and selfless act in the world. According to this principle, there definitely isn't. Even giving to charity would in some way bring pleasure or avoid pain. No matter what we do in the course of our day, it all gets down to the pleasure principle. You get a haircut because you think it will make you more attractive to someone else, which will make you happy, which is pleasure.

Conversely, you wear a protective mask while you're using a blowtorch because you want to avoid sparks flying into your face and eyes, because that will be painful. If you trace all of our decisions back, whether short-term or long-term, you'll find that they all stem from a small set of pleasures or pains.

> *Self-discipline corollary: doing what we need to do is often painful and devoid of pleasure, so we don't do it.*

People work harder to avoid pain than to get pleasure. Your behaviors will skew toward pain avoidance more than pleasure-seeking. The instinct to survive a threatening situation is more immediate than eating your favorite candy bar, for instance. You would rather avoid getting punched in the face than drink your favorite whiskey.

> *Self-discipline corollary: giving up is often less painful than persevering. So we give up.*

Our perceptions of pleasure and pain are more powerful drivers than the actual things. When our brain is judging between what will be a pleasant or painful experience, it's working from scenarios that we *think* could result if we took a course of action. And sometimes those scenarios can be flawed. In fact, they are *mostly* flawed.

For instance, you might be deathly afraid of heights. Skydiving would naturally be your worst nightmare. It is for me, anyway.

You might have no idea how it feels. You have probably never gone bungee-jumping or even ridden a roller-coaster. Perhaps the most you've tested your fear of heights is standing on the balcony of your two-story house. But the *thought* of jumping out of a plane makes you physically nauseous. You imagine how the feeling of weightlessness is a precursor to death. You imagine that you will indeed die.

But *you haven't actually tried it.* All you have are perceptions and assumptions, and that's enough to magnify the pain of skydiving to extremes. Incidentally, skydiving has an incredibly low rate of accidents and is over within a series of minutes. Your brain deals in the business of worst-case scenarios.

> *Self-discipline corollary: unfamiliarity breeds fear, which breeds avoidance. So you avoid acting.*

Pleasure and pain are changed by time. In general, we focus on the here and now: what can I get very soon that will bring me happiness? Also, what is coming up very soon that could be painful and I'll have to avoid? Immediacy is king. One dollar right now is far more attractive than five dollars in one month's time.

The pleasure and pain that might happen months or years from now don't really register with us—what's most important is whatever's right at our doorstep. This certainly doesn't help our sense of planning for the future if we are stuck in the present moment.

> *Self-discipline corollary: the rewards we seek are rarely immediate, and often, the longer-term they are, the greater they are. But we're stuck in the now, so we avoid action.*

Emotion beats logic. When it comes to the pleasure principle, your feelings tend to overshadow rational thought. You might know that doing something will be good or bad for you. You'll understand all the reasons why it will be good or bad. You get all that.

But then an emotional impulse rears its head and screams, "So what?!" There's nothing you can do to control the power of a volcano, even if you know it's within your control. Losing a dollar might be bad on its own, but when you insert emotion into this loss, it stops becoming about the dollar, and more about everything the dollar could possibly represent, and then you're headed down a slippery slope.

Self-discipline corollary: logic doesn't control our behavior nearly as much as we would like to believe it does.

At this point, you should see the writing on the wall that the pleasure principle is one of the main saboteurs of self-discipline. We've always been biologically wired to not think ahead and care most about the present moment—essentially the opposite of what self-discipline focuses on. This is the same reason that delaying gratification is difficult. However, we can skirt around this by changing the way we think about pleasure and pain.

In the pursuit of self-discipline, we want to increase the pleasure in every long-term duty or obligation we have and lessen the pain. There are a series of steps we can use to do this strategically.

1. Decide what you want. What is your goal that requires self-discipline? It can be as simple as working out more.

2. Take inventory of your pain and pleasure. This is where you take aspects of the pleasure principle and start massaging them to your benefit. Here's what you do:

- Take two sheets of paper. Draw a line down the middle of each page.

- At the top of the left column on both pages, write down "PAIN AVOIDED."

- At the top of the right column on both pages, write down "PLEASURE GAINED."

- Now, at the top-center of one of the pages, write down "BEING DISCIPLINED."

- At the top-center of the other pages, write down "NOT BEING DISCIPLINED."

By now you probably know what we're up to. You're going to list the pain and pleasure you expect you'll experience when you take a step toward accomplishing your goal or when you decide not to. To motivate yourself psychologically, you're going to ramp up the pain associated with *not being* disciplined, and the pleasure associated with *being* disciplined. This may seem elementary, but it's a level of perspective and insight that you can use to combat your impulses. Just taking stock of what happens in reality can help quell your impulses.

For example, let's take that goal of working out more. Let's go with the "NOT BEING DISCIPLINED" bit first. It might look something like this:

NOT BEING DISCIPLINED to work out more	
PAIN AVOIDED	PLEASURE GAINED
Embarrassment, shame at gym	More television time
No sore muscles	More free time in general
Paying gym fees	

Now let's make one up for "BEING DISCIPLINED":

BEING DISCIPLINED to work out more	
PAIN AVOIDED	PLEASURE GAINED
Feeling lazy	Confidence
Lack of dates	Attractiveness
High blood pressure	Real-world strength

List as many pain and pleasure points as you can for each scenario. Be honest with yourself and try to think the potential through as much as you can. You should get some clarity about what your aspirations and ambitions are—not to mention your hopes and fears.

3. Tip the scales in your favor. This is a part where you get creative. Take the "NOT BEING DISCIPLINED" sheet and minimize the pains. They are minor; they are trivial. Convince yourself that these small things shouldn't have such power over you. Tip the scales in your favor, so to speak.

Now, for the "BEING DISCIPLINED" sheet, amplify the pleasures. Picture how utterly fantastic each of these situations could turn out. Think about the best-case scenarios that could result with each of these items. Take the positive possibilities and run with them. Don't be surprised if you get a minor dopamine rush from this alone.

This sheet is more than just an inventory: it's a checklist for reinforcing your self-discipline. What you have just done is created a very tangible cost-benefit analysis that gets to the heart of what makes you act. Instead of waiting for our prehistoric brain to sabotage our efforts because of the lack of pie or television, we can tip the scales a bit in our favor when it comes to dopamine and make our brain work *for* us rather than against us.

Time Orientation

Another influence on the level of self-discipline we have in our lives involves our relationship with time—not in the sense of scheduling or "making time," but how we reflect, act, and react with the notions of past, present, and future.

With time orientation, in Stanford Professor Phil Zimbardo's (the professor best known for the Stanford prison experiment) book *The Time Paradox*, it is theorized that each of us can view time in one of three ways: past, present, and future. Our psyches tend to frame our experience using whatever orientation we're most acclimated to. Put simply, there are actual differences between those of us who are mired in nostalgia, versus those who are continually looking for the next step in life.

Whatever time orientation our mindset reflects relates to how we expect and plan for rewards, which feeds into how self-disciplined we may be. More specifically, our attitudes toward the present and future come squarely into play.

The past-oriented person makes all their decisions from historical information or recall, and by definition they are generally separated from current situations or events. People stuck in the past don't have much use for the new and different, regarding them with suspicion, disdain, or even prejudice. Their thinking is almost inactive—which is not conducive to self-discipline. They will say, "Well, this is what I did in the past, so I'll just keep doing that." However, this type of thought is extremely rare, and we will spend more time on future- and present-oriented people.

Someone who focuses on the present lives primarily in "the now." They react most powerfully to what their senses are showing them at the moment. They tend to be very concrete in their thinking, choosing to orient themselves toward "what is" rather than what happened in the past or what could happen in the future. The "present" mindset can be broken down even further into two distinct camps: those who embrace the possibilities of the present (we'll call them "hedonists") and those who don't like the present but feel they have no other choice but to live in it (we'll call them "fatalists").

The present-hedonistic person finds opportunities in the current time and is happy to indulge in what's happening around them now. They're the ones who go to parties, embrace adventures in unfamiliar places, or interact with society on an ongoing basis. They're happy to take risks and don't necessarily care too much about the consequences (or have plans to mitigate the results if they have to).

The present-fatalist person doesn't *really* want to be focused on the present, but they don't feel the future holds anything for them. They sense that somebody or something else—whether it's their social circle, financial realities, religion, or "luck"—is in control of their lives and consider the whole game of existence to be "rigged." Their expectations and hopes have been dashed, and they don't feel any need to work for the future because they don't believe they have one.

What both of the present mindsets have in common is their attitude toward *gratification.* Since the past and the future don't come to mind, all that matters is momentary and fleeting pleasure. Both hedonists and fatalists are oriented toward the notion of *instant* gratification.

Which one of these present mindsets is more suited to the process of building self-discipline? Neither of them.

Self-discipline and instant gratification are opposing ideas. Self-discipline confers what instant gratification can never bring about: patience, restraint, full understanding, planning, responsibility. When you're oriented toward immediate reward, none of those other things matter.

This is an appropriate time to invoke the fable of the ant and the grasshopper. Briefly speaking, the ant worked long and hard all year and never faltered from storing food and preparing for winter. The ant always knew what would matter in the long-term. The grasshopper, however, only did enough to get by day to day and didn't think about the winter. He only thought about maximizing his pleasure in the moment. When winter came, the ants fared just fine, if not annoyed at eating the same thing for months on end. The grasshopper starved from a lack of preparation.

Present-oriented people are the grasshopper, while future-oriented people are ants. And you can guess which time orientation is more conducive to self-discipline.

Those with *future* mindsets frame their lives differently. They aren't bound strictly to what the present has to offer (or deny) them. They are able to disconnect from it; concrete and empirical reality doesn't bind them. They focus on the future with all its distant possibilities and consequences.

The future-oriented first think about the outcome they want, then work backward to how their actions create it. They do so without the distractions of the present. And even though they frequently work with abstract ideas and no guarantee of positive results, they still organize their thoughts and actions toward fulfillment of some future goal.

In other words, the future-oriented have no problem with *delayed* gratification. They don't need instant affirmation or reward for their efforts. They understand that what's most important to them might take a little time to develop. Sometimes that means working in something that feels like a vacuum (or might *seem* like a vacuum to someone living in the present). But all it means is that the futurist is willing to forsake immediate satisfaction *now* for a more fulfilling and meaningful satisfaction *later*—possibly.

That mindset is perfectly suited to someone with strong self-discipline. The futurist develops patience as a plank of their long-range planning. They keep the greater goal in mind rather than the annoyances that eventually get them there. This meshes well with other research on the matter showing that thinking about a literal future version of you is helpful in adhering to habits and accomplishing goals.

Let's talk about this in terms of baseball. Most, if not all, baseball teams are under immense pressure from owners and fans to win *now*, which leads them to trade away some of their minor-league prospects for proven players who might be able to lead them to the promised land for a season or two. Sometimes it works, and the team makes the playoffs or might even win a championship. But they don't stay on top for too long because they dealt away too many of their future players for the one big gun that will help them win next week.

But some teams—most recently the Houston Astros—spend a few years taking their lumps with players they developed with an eye toward the future. Their process was so unusual that *Sports Illustrated* did a cover story on the Astros in 2014: "Baseball's Great Experiment: Your 2017 World Series Champs." The Astros wanted to build a core of great players that could help them contend on an annual basis, not just in a one-and-done scenario where they have a one- or two-year window.

So, they built up their farm system (their minor-league developing players) to sharpen and develop their skills, keeping them together through years of patience and losing, before they finally bloomed into a contending team with players they didn't cast off for the big shiny object. This set them back considerably in the short-term but paid off in the end. It required great discipline to not give in to temptations to stem the short-term pain.

Such teams are built for long periods of success, and for the Astros, it brought them a World Series championship—in the year 2017, exactly as *SI* had predicted.

It should be noted most of us are a blend of present and future-oriented thinking. This means that we end up with two distinct selves that we have to attend to and keep satisfied. They are quite aptly summed up with the hedonist grasshopper (present) and blue-collar ant (future) from earlier. If you compromise the two equally, it results in an ant that takes breaks while diligently working toward a goal and the grasshopper that realizes that discomfort is required in life. That's really the best we can expect in everyday life.

The concept of time orientations should force you to consider and skew your view toward the future. Future you is trying to build a foundation for *their* success. He's the one that has your best interests in mind. Self-discipline is an irreplaceable part of that foundation.

It's Up to You

The obstacles to self-discipline as we've outlined them so far might seem like a big load to handle. And they are; most people never break through any of them and it reflects in their lives. You yourself might be wondering if it's beyond your reach or capabilities: "Am I really capable of breaking through and developing the willpower I need to do what I need to do?"

As the saying goes, "Whether you think you can or you can't, you're right." When it comes to developing willpower, the most important factor might not be your mental or physical abilities or the range of what you can accomplish. Rather, it may simply be your *belief* that you can develop willpower.

A study by researcher Veronika Job examined university students over a single scholastic term. Job asked the students to evaluate themselves on their ability to maintain willpower over the course of a given task—whether they need to take a break after a run of tough work or whether their endurance "fueled itself" and allowed them to keep going.

Across the board, the students who believed that their willpower was unlimited did better in several measures. They regulated their activities better, kept procrastination at bay, got better grades, and were even better at eating right and maintaining physical health. On the other side, students who said they needed to recharge themselves from time to time were especially beset by procrastination, often made poor dietary decisions, and found themselves easily distracted. They even spent more money—theoretically while they were distracting themselves with online destinations.

Job's results indicated that those students who were convinced of their own abilities and really *believed* they had more willpower actually *did.* Their self-messaging turned out to be a crucial element in their superior performance, to the point where it couldn't simply be coincidence. Score another point for the placebo effect.

This is great news because it implies that although building willpower is a challenge, a huge part of the solution is simply believing that you can do it. We have exactly as much willpower as we think we do.

Building self-discipline is your choice and yours alone—it's all up to you. Nobody and nothing else have as much influence in the attainment of your goals. It doesn't matter how your brain is wired or where you are oriented with regards to time. What overrides those is your belief in yourself.

Ultimately, this ends up being a good thing because it places the power in your hands. Whether you can or cannot be disciplined is up to you. For some, this is a freeing thought to determine one's behavior and actions. By producing your own incentive and making self-discipline its own reward, you'll see positive effects unveil themselves on a daily, gradual basis. These benefits include the following, which you can also feel free to factor into your pleasure principle cost-benefit analysis.

Avoiding temptation. The self-disciplined mind knows that fighting temptation is a Herculean task. Even the strongest-minded person might feel a tinge of enticement when they're walking past the window of an ice cream shop where there's a huge color display of a towering sundae hanging in the window. Unless you hate ice cream, you'll feel a twinge.

But what self-discipline helps you do is *avoid* the temptation—pass the shop by without feeling the need to indulge. This is because self-discipline helps you control and direct yourself when there are clashing internal forces at work. Your mind won't focus on the deprivation aspect: it'll concentrate on the good you're producing.

More life satisfaction. Those who practice self-discipline frequently report that they're happier than people who don't. This reality flies in the face the idea that self-discipline means not having any fun. What you're trying to get on the pathway of self-control will be a thousand times more gratifying than the rewards of an immediate thrill— it's just going to take a little longer.

Patience can be frustrating. When you live in a society like we do, where instant pleasure is relatively easy to pursue, it can *really* be hard to walk a line of restraint and control, especially when you have friends who constantly live for the moment. But what you're after is bigger than that: you want to create a more satisfying and contented *lifetime*. That's something that only self-discipline and continued focus will bring. When it does, it'll be much more meaningful and satisfying than those brief, isolated diversions.

You do more of what you want. On a similar note, those who take up a life of self-discipline are often imagined as "not doing" things. They're not up to date on the current hit TV shows; they're not hanging out with their bar friends on a nightly basis; they're not traveling to Fort Lauderdale on spring break. In some way or another, they're perceived as being left out—but that's only according to other people's concept of fun.

In reality, the self-disciplined person is giving themselves more opportunity to do what they *actually* want to do. This comes about in two ways. First, you have the ability to position yourself for success and do what needs to be done. This leaves time for the interests you want to pursue, and it can even be just a lazy afternoon of television.

Second, you have the discipline to do *challenging* things that you want. You might want to climb a set of mountains or run a marathon. Self-discipline is how you do them. They're doing activities that are rewarding and enriching—and they're doing them because they've disciplined themselves to be able to do them and appreciate them.

You gain ultimate freedom.

Actually, you're MORE in the moment. Taking the road to self-discipline is a constant process that frequently requires you to make choices. You need to be fully aware of the decisions that can help you the most. Sometimes opportunities will arise out of nowhere: a chance to talk with someone who's been down your path before and can give you some advice or support or an activity like yoga that can help you develop more mental stamina and concentration.

These opportunities seem to arise for people who are working on self-discipline, but it's not magic. It's because you're more aware and attuned to things that will help you get to where you want to go. The self-disciplined mind isn't shut off—far from it. It's looking for and recognizing those chances all the time. You're *more* aware of what's happening around you. You're not missing anything. You're just making a different choice.

Setting boundaries. Chances are, you have at least one or two good friends or relations who will be thrilled to support you in any way they can. But let's face it: there will also be a few of them who will try—knowingly or otherwise—to knock you off your path to self-discipline. "C'mon, you can miss a gym session. There's beer and a game of *Call of Duty* with your name on it."

Self-discipline helps you identify those conflicts before they begin and can make you stand your ground. It can also build your resolve to resist the pleadings and guilt-tripping of others who might not be that understanding of your goal to improve yourself.

Knowing yourself. Finally, self-discipline is one of the best ways to find out who you really are and what you really value—in a real-world setting. At times, our situations can seem so bothersome or troubling that we can't imagine any course other than escape. But in those scenarios, you're not just escaping hardship or the world: you're also escaping *yourself.*

Self-discipline is a means to reject the traits of reaction and retreat. It gives you something to actively work on every day and forces you to make decisions and take actions based on what you really need. Through that process, you *will* learn more about yourself than you ever have before. You'll see why you made certain decisions in the past, and you'll understand what kind of person you really are.

Takeaways:

- Self-discipline is the act of putting mind over matter and dictating exactly what your actions and behaviors are. But control over the mind is like saying you want to take a casual stroll to the surface of the sun. It's not easy and must be reined in constantly for you to even have a chance of self-discipline. As it turns out, there are many obstacles to acting disciplined and controlling yourself.
- Buddhism teaches five mental hindrances to self-discipline: giving in to the five senses, animosity and malice, apathy and laziness, anxiety and remorse, and hesitation and doubt. The common thread is that they all require immediate and urgent attention, even if it is fabricated urgency. When you are so

focused on the now, the *later* that self-discipline serves becomes wholly unimportant.

- Another aspect of being unable to move past the present moment and plan for the future is how the neurotransmitter dopamine influences our actions. Humans abide by the pleasure principle; we seek pleasure and avoid pain whenever possible, even subconsciously. Acting self-disciplined very rarely brings you pleasure, and most of the time it actively brings some measure of pain or at least discomfort. That's a problem. We must change the way we think about pleasure and pain, and who we want to benefit the most: in most cases, your future self.

- Time orientation is yet another problem with self-discipline. Some of us are present-oriented—this will not serve you well because you won't be able to act in the best interests of future you. Others of us are future-oriented—we think about what we want in the future and work backward to create it. This perspective meshes much better with self-discipline. In the fable of the ant and the grasshopper, the diligent ant is future-oriented and survives the winter, while the hedonistic grasshopper is present-oriented and starves.

- In the end, despite all these obstacles, whether or not you have self-discipline is up to you. This is in a literal sense— the placebo effect has shown that however much you believe you have, that's what you'll have. This is empowering and freeing because it means there is nothing between you and what you want—besides you. It's up to you. This is actually ultimate freedom, not restriction, as self-discipline is sometimes framed. Take it as a challenge to be overcome.

Chapter 2. Understand the Cycle; Break the Cycle

Whenever you have a mental lapse and suffer a breach in self-discipline, it might seem like an isolated incident. Perhaps it was simply due to one of the obstacles in the previous chapter holding you back. *It's all due to the time orientation you possess, and once you fix that, you'll be fine.*

Most of us process losing our willpower at this basic level; we lost control momentarily because of a one-off occurrence, and we only realize after the fact that we were avoiding exercising our self-discipline.

We knew we had to wash the car that day, but we just *never got around to it*. Is that something that just tends to happen from time to time, or is there something deeper at play here? Unfortunately, it doesn't come close to telling the whole story, and the deeper we go, the closer we get to what happens when you are robbed of self-discipline.

Moving higher on the ladder of awareness, some of us might have identified a couple of specific triggers that cause us to lose our self-discipline, and thus we avoid them consciously. We *know* we hate washing the car, and we *know* we find excuses to be out of the house until someone else washes it (or until the next rainy day comes). This is still not the whole story, but it is helpful to know what is motivating you one way or the other.

The next level of awareness in our self-discipline failures might be the recognition that there are specific behaviors you engage in whenever you avoid it. For instance, you notice that when you want to avoid washing your car you start cleaning your room instead. Psychological discomfort is created because you know you are avoiding your responsibilities, so you engage in a distraction to alleviate that discomfort. Eventually, this would allow you to see a pattern that if you are cleaning your room, perhaps the car, or something even more important, is being avoided at the moment.

It may not be immediately clear, but there is a cycle that, if you lack self-discipline, you will constantly find yourself in. You might be able to "push through it" from time to time, but that's not something you should have to rely on for your whole life. The sustainable path to self-discipline involves identifying and breaking the cycle of lacking self-discipline.

The Cycle of Laziness

In some ways, the existence of a cycle is a relief because this means self-discipline isn't so much about putting mind over matter and grinding past the pain (although sometimes that part cannot be avoided). Neither is the key to self-discipline about endless affirmations and other such statements—it's actually about understanding the cycle of laziness and disrupting it before you get sucked into it.

It's the equivalent of understanding how to use a certain physics equation to solve a problem, versus trying to solve the problem differently each time, and sometimes just trying out twenty different possibilities. When you know what you're looking for, you're just going to be far more effective. In practical terms, this means that doing what you need to do will be much less of a struggle in the end.

The level of analysis in the earlier example about not possessing the self-discipline to wash a car is deeper than most people ever get, as they only think in terms of two mental modes: feeling apathetic or feeling adequately energized. This is too simplistic to explain what self-discipline really consists of. And so long as you don't really acknowledge what's happening on deeper levels, you'll continue to say things like, "I didn't get around to it," and write off lapses as temporary, unavoidable slip-ups and nothing more.

There are five main phases of the cycle that explain why you tend to keep sitting on your butt, even though you know you shouldn't be. But perhaps more importantly, it further explains how you *justify* sitting on your butt, and even how you'll probably sit on your butt even more decisively the next time. We can follow along with the same example of car washing.

- Unhelpful assumptions or made-up rules: "Life is short, so I should enjoy it and not spend my precious time washing that dusty car! Car washes are something you pay for anyway!"
- Increasing discomfort: "I'd rather not wash the car. It's boring and uncomfortable. I know my spouse asked me to, but it can wait."
- Excuses for lack of self-discipline to decrease psychological discomfort: "It's perfectly reasonable for me not to wash the car. It's so hot outside I would melt. My spouse didn't really mean it when they asked."
- Avoidance activities to decrease psychological discomfort: "I will clean the bathroom instead. I'm still productive! I'll also arrange my desk. Lots of things getting done today. I did pretty well today, all things considered."

- Negative and positive consequences: "Ah, I feel better about myself now. Cleanliness all around. Oh, wait. I still need to wash that car, and my spouse seems angrier this time . . ."

Which brings us full circle right back to the start: the car isn't washed, and your assumptions remain the same. Only this time, there's even more discomfort that you want to avoid immediately. And so it goes on. Your discomfort chases you round and round, and you pretend to avoid it, only to find it pop up somewhere else. Once you're in the cycle, it's hard to get over the increasing inertia keeping you from getting the task done. The looming chore of washing the car hangs over you, seeming to get bigger and more awful the longer it goes on not being completed . . .

Let's take a look at each of the phases individually, and then you'll start to understand why it's so essential to interrupt this cycle. We'll start right from the top; this is where you are either failing to start a task, or to complete a task already underway. You know logically that you should do these things, and they are in your best interests. However, you've already made the decision against self-discipline, so what goes through your mind? Or rather, what has happened already, without your conscious awareness?

Unhelpful Assumptions or Made-Up Rules

If you feel like you don't want to start or follow through with something, it's not due to simple laziness or "I don't feel like it right now." It's about the (usually unquestioned and unchallenged) beliefs and assumptions that underlie these feelings. What are some of these unhelpful assumptions or made-up rules?

My life should be about seeking pleasure, having fun, and enjoying myself. Anything that conflicts with that shouldn't be allowed. We all fall into this at one time or another. Pleasure-seeking is where you feel that life is too short to pass up something fun, interesting, or pleasant in favor of things that may seem boring or hard. Fun is the priority! At the very least, you believe that the current short-term pleasure is more important than a long-term payoff.

This is the true meaning of "I don't feel like it right now"—you are actually saying, "I want to do something more pleasurable than that right now."

I need X, Y, or Z to exercise my self-discipline, and if they are not present, I am excused. Sometimes you just can't muster up the energy to do something. You may feel tired, stressed, depressed, or unmotivated and use that as your "reason" for not getting things done. You have to be "ready." You need X, Y, and Z to start properly. You have to be in the mood. Oops! The stars aren't magically aligned, so you can't do as you said you would, and it's not even really your fault.

All these so-called requirements were conjured by *you*, though; none of them actually reflect reality. Nobody is putting any hurdles between you and the task. And sometimes you do need to push through until fatigue and exhaustion hit—self-discipline isn't about the easy path. You *will* be uncomfortable, so don't assume that you shouldn't be (this goes back to the first assumption, i.e. that life is always meant to feel good, so if you're uncomfortable, something is going wrong and you need to stop what you're doing at once).

I probably won't do it right, so I just won't do it at all. You may fall into the assumption that you must do things perfectly every time or else it will be labeled a failure. This is a fear of failure and rejection, and it also involves a lack of self-confidence. You also don't want others to think less of you. You might call this "being a perfectionist," but it's really a lack of courage and resilience. It's actually you believing deep down that you cannot or won't endure any difficulties—either the thing goes perfectly or you will simply not attempt it (sounds kind of bratty when put that way, doesn't it?).

And how do you ensure that you don't get rejected or fail at a task? You don't do it. Easy. You don't start it, and you don't finish it. There won't be failure or disappointment because you don't allow the opportunity for judgment.

I alone dictate what I do. This is where you assume that you need to be the one to call the shots and to be in control. You feel a strong attachment to being in charge. You feel you shouldn't have to do something just because someone *tells* you to. This is best summed up by the statement: "I don't have to listen to them." This is a defensive reaction to what you view as someone stepping on you, and it often leads to you acting against your own interests. It doesn't matter if you yourself have set that goal or expectation—the instant you do, you reflexively push back as though in a bid for your perceived freedom.

If you feel that you need to do something that goes against your beliefs, you will only do it when absolutely necessary. This is a reality of human behavior, as is the fact that these beliefs are usually unconscious. So, what happens if you are told to do household chores but you possess the first two beliefs of "fun comes first" and "I need perfect conditions"? You'll have fun first, wait for a large set of preconditions, and the chores will go undone. The rest of the cycle is what *keeps* them undone.

Increasing Discomfort

How do you know whether you possess any of the above assumptions or core beliefs? When you know you are supposed to exercise self-discipline, yet it conflicts with a belief or assumption of yours, tension and discomfort will be created. This happens because there is a direct conflict between what you desire (no car washing!) and what the world (or an individual, or even yourself) is telling you (just wash it for once).

Imagine being told that the sky is actually red, which probably conflicts with what you've been taught since childhood. You feel that something is amiss, but you might not be able to put a name to it. You will have a range of emotions, all of which are uncomfortable: anger, boredom, frustration, exhaustion, resentment, anxiety, embarrassment, fear, or despair. Let's call them all a variation of psychological discomfort. They point to a mismatch between the external world and your inner beliefs about it.

The end result of this conflict is that we are in an agitated state, and *we don't like feeling that way*. So, something will need to change.

If the source of this discomfort is anything having to do with washing that darned car, that means you're going to avoid it like the black plague.

We know it still exists, but we are in the beginnings of rationalizing why we shouldn't or don't need to do it. Think of it this way: your brain doesn't want you to stay in a state of psychological discomfort—it's like standing on the bow of a sinking ship—so it deals with it the only way it knows how through the next two phases.

Making Excuses

Excuses are what you use to make yourself feel better when you are ducking responsibility. You know you should do something, but you don't want to. Does this mean you're just lazy, tired, or entitled to no action? Of course not. Admitting those would cause even more discomfort and tension than you already feel. So you construct excuses to remain the good guy or even victim in your situation—or at least not the bad guy. Now that's a comforting thought. What would you say to make your lack of action acceptable?

"I don't want to miss out on that party tonight. I'll do it tomorrow."

"I'm just too tired tonight. I'll start working on that goal later."

"I'll do a better job on that project when I'm in the mood to work on it."

"I don't have everything I need to finish the job, so I can't start now."

"I'll do it right after I finish this other task."

Now, if you uttered these to someone else, they might reply with a raised eyebrow and a, "Really . . .?" The problem is, these excuses are ones that you tell yourself. And you've probably used them so frequently in your life that the lines between your excuses and reality have blurred. You become unable to discern or tell the truth, and you unknowingly start to disempower yourself. Remember, we possess the amount of self-discipline that we believe we possess. Excuses tell you that you are easily defeated. It's almost note even relevant whether the excuses are believable or not—they are simply there to relieve discomfort and give you an "out."

And while you're busy convincing yourself that these excuses are real and legitimate, you are smoothly transitioning into the next phase in the cycle: avoidance activities.

Avoidance Activities

Avoidance activities are the culmination of alleviating your discomfort and wanting to feel like you aren't simply being lazy. The internal dialogue goes something like this: "I'm sufficiently justified in not washing the car, but why do I still feel lousy about myself? I should do something . . ." Excuses on their own may not be enough, so you figure some action is still needed to lessen the discomfort and tension.

And so you act, though it's never what you should be doing in the first place. Typically, there are two types of avoidance activities. First, there are activities that simply distract you from the discomfort of choosing not to exercise your self-discipline or violate a belief or assumption. Out of sight, out of mind, and the discomfort is destroyed by going for ice cream or to a new superhero movie. This is distraction to the point of denial.

Second, there are activities that make you feel productive in some other way than the task at hand. For instance, if you work from home and are putting off a project, you will never have a cleaner bathroom than when real tasks are to be avoided. You might do an "easier" or lower-priority task. These avoidance activities allow you to say, "Well, at least I did something and wasn't totally unproductive with my time!" A fitting term for these activities is *productive procrastination*.

These activities do help you feel better about yourself in the short-term, but they don't move you any closer to where you should be, and make the cycle harder to break. That psychological discomfort is still there.

Negative and Positive Consequences

Avoiding is an art. But when you avoid responsibilities, there are always consequences. Somewhere, something is slipping through the cracks. The negative consequences are more obvious. You've probably experienced them all before. They can include increased discomfort, guilt, anxiety, and shame. You know you're not achieving (or taking steps to achieve) your goal, and this just makes you feel worse.

Another negative consequence is having increased demands on you. Your work may accumulate, leaving you to have to do the original task plus the additional compensatory work. And depending on the nature of the task, avoidance may lead to a consequence of punishment or loss. That punishment/loss may be in the form of repercussions at work, a missed opportunity, or failing to meet a goal. The chores go undone, and your lawn gets so out of control that you start to find small, vicious woodland animals in it.

Other negative consequences are related to this very cycle, where your unhelpful or incorrect assumptions or beliefs remain unchallenged, you become overly effective at making excuses for yourself, and your tolerance for psychological discomfort shrinks even more. These all perpetuate the cycle even worse. And you may be completely unaware that any of this is going on, still ignorant of *why you can't just do the thing already.*

Any positive consequences are illusory. They may be positive in that they feel good in the moment, but they are temporary at best. It's like shutting your eyes to avoid the bright headlights of a truck barreling toward you—you are just setting yourself up for failure in the long term. It's self-sabotage.

Avoidance lets you move away from that initial discomfort you were feeling about *not* doing the task. You may actually feel better because you are sticking to your unhelpful assumptions. And you will probably get some enjoyment from your procrastination activities. Both of these could be considered a positive consequence of putting off the task.

Both sets of consequences contribute to furthering the cycle. Negative consequences make you want to continue avoiding certain tasks, while positive consequences inject just enough short-term pleasure to disguise what's really happening. And they both lead you right back to the initial problem of lacking self-discipline. Whether you're motivated by the negative consequence or the positive consequence, the outcome is the same: you are less likely to complete your task or goal.

You can now see how this can become a vicious cycle. The more you subscribe to one or more of the unhelpful assumptions, the greater your discomfort. With increasing discomfort, you start to make excuses to avoid. The more you avoid, the more you *want* to avoid it due to both the negative and positive consequences. And you start back in with the unhelpful assumptions—probably strengthened for the worse at this point.

So what do these phases look like in a day-to-day life situation? Let's walk through the familiar chain reaction of events that you have unwittingly followed for years. Let's take the illustrative example of weight loss.

You are likely operating under several unhelpful assumptions. You think you can't lose weight unless you give up all pleasure and become a monk. What if you can't lose the weight? What if you can't keep it off? It's just easier to keep doing what you're doing rather than risking failure. Another assumption you may have is that you lack energy and time. You're just too tired to go cook for yourself and exercise every day; it's easier just to grab fast food.

These unhelpful assumptions then lead to discomfort. What feelings are causing you to feel uncomfortable? Maybe you feel bad about eating something you know you shouldn't. Maybe you're jealous that your sister can just eat what she wants. Maybe you're irritated that fresh fruits and vegetables are so expensive. Maybe you feel embarrassed because you haven't lost weight at all despite secretly starting to care about your goal. You can't carry on in the status quo, so something needs to change.

So, you start to soften the discomfort by making excuses. You don't have the right workout clothes to go to the gym. You don't want to miss out on the birthday party fun, so you're going to have that piece of cake. You're too tired after work to do all that meal prep. You'll just wait for the beginning of the month so you can track everything more neatly.

Deep down inside, you may or may not realize these are excuses to keep you in inaction. But whatever the case, you will eventually feel that some sort of action is required. This is where avoidance activities come in. Remember, there are two types: ones that distract you from your growing discomfort and ones that make you feel like you're doing something (though you really aren't).

Maybe you go out for dinner with coworkers after work instead of going to the gym. You might spend time finding recipes on Pinterest instead of actually cooking a healthy meal. Maybe you hop on the Internet to intensely and painstakingly research what kind of gym equipment you need instead of just going to the gym.

These actions lead to consequences. One negative consequence could be feelings of guilt: guilt for not working out, guilt for not following a meal plan, guilt about the choices you're making. Another negative consequence could be actually gaining weight instead of losing it.

The only positive consequences are related to not delaying gratification and being able to pretend that you are doing everything correctly. Another positive could be that your "cheat meal" improved your mood.

Negative consequences lead to more avoidance and lack of desire to face reality. Positive consequences lead to more self-sabotage. And now you're back to the beginning with even less incentive or optimism about losing weight.

Let's look at another example.

What if you've always wanted to open an ice cream shop? Your friends and family know you love ice cream, and you're always talking about this dream of yours, but you've never taken the plunge to start your own business. Maybe there's a cycle of lack of self-discipline contributing to your hesitancy to open that shop.

Jumping into the cycle, what are the unhelpful assumptions you're telling yourself? A prime assumption would be fear of the unknown or catastrophe. If you quit your job and go full speed ahead with your ice cream business, what if it fails? What will it be like to be a business owner? What if you lose a ton of money? You may also suffer from a lack of self-confidence. What if you *can't* do this? You tell yourself you don't have the business acumen, you've never done this before, and you have no idea what you're doing.

Another unhelpful assumption you may be making is that you need to be in charge. Now, it might seem that, with your own business, you *would* be in charge. But there are things out of your control. Your business loan is dependent on the banker. You won't have ice cream to sell if your supplier can't get your product to you. You can't guarantee that you'll have customers. These are all things out of your control.

Thinking about these assumptions probably has you feeling pretty uncomfortable. You likely have some anxiety about such a big change. There may be some fear mixed in at the thought of quitting your job to go out on your own. You may be feeling overwhelmed by all the things that go into starting your own business.

When you're feeling this uncomfortable, it's easy to come up with excuses for not moving forward. You can't open an ice cream shop because you just don't have the know-how. Maybe your excuse is that you don't know for sure if your shop will be a success. Or perhaps you feel like you don't have time to open a business.

So as a result of these excuses, you move into avoidance activities. Instead of going to the bank to find out about business loans, you watch the football game on TV instead. You get distracted. Or you get together with friends to talk about your idea instead of taking action on steps to move toward your dream. You feel productive in some non-movement way.

As for consequences of these avoidance tactics? One negative consequence may be that you miss out on an opportunity for a perfect location for your ice cream shop because you hadn't moved forward with your plan. One positive consequence could be that you enjoy spending time with your friends and you like talking about your idea, leading you to do this more frequently instead of starting up your business. Again, negative consequences create pessimism, while positive consequences create self-sabotage.

And here we are again at the start of the cycle. You lack the self-discipline to start your new business because you are operating under unhelpful assumptions, which cause you to make excuses that lead to avoidance that, in turn, results in consequences that hamper your self-discipline.

It's time to talk about breaking the cycle. Fortunately, a cycle doesn't need to be broken in any particular location or sequence. Once any phase is disrupted, it makes the rest impossible to continue.

Breaking the Cycle

Remember that the cycle of lacking self-discipline has five phases. In this section, we talk about exactly how to address each of the first four phases.

One. Unhelpful assumptions or made-up rules: "Life is short. I should enjoy it and not spend my precious time washing that dusty car! Car washes are something you pay for, anyway!"

To clear up any unhelpful assumptions regarding self-discipline, consider something of a favorite concept of mine: the forty percent rule.

It says that when an individual's mind begins telling them that they are physically or emotionally maxed out, in reality they have only pushed themselves to forty percent of their full capacity. In other words, they could endure sixty percent more if only they believed that they were capable of it. When you think you have reached your limits, you're not even close, and whether you can keep going or not depends on if you believe it. It's quite a belief to feel that you've reached your limits and say to yourself that you're only forty percent done. It's an acceptance of pain, and that's a belief that is much more beneficial to your self-discipline.

What if you were to replace your unhelpful, disempowering assumptions with this one of strength and agency?

We are usually ready to give up around the time that we begin to feel pain or are barely pressing our boundaries. But that point is actually just the beginning of what we are all capable of, and the key to unlocking more potential is to push through the initial pain and the self-doubt that surfaces along with it. By maintaining a belief in yourself, you show yourself that you can do more, and that evidence builds your confidence and discipline.

You might, for example, begin struggling after doing ten push-ups. You'd start hearing the voice in your head that says you feel too tired, too sore, or too weak to go on. But if you take a pause and gather yourself to do one more, you find that you've already disproven the voice saying that you can't. Then you pause and do another. And then another.

And then another. Suddenly, you're at twenty. You can take it slowly, but you've just doubled what you thought was possible.

Believing that you can do more will make it true. It enables you to go well beyond the limits that you've constructed for yourself in your own mind. And once you've felt the pain and the urge to give up at ten push-ups only to push through it and do twenty, you know that your mental strength helped you persevere. The next time you're challenged, you'll feel all the more capable and prepared to push past your supposed limits again. This embodies self-discipline in a nutshell—it's really a matter of how much pain you can stomach, and most of us will only bend and never break.

Our minds can be our best friends when we have a strong belief in our capabilities, but they can also be a poisonous enemy if we allow negativity to seize control. It's up to you to empower yourself using the forty percent rule rather than throwing in the towel mentally at the first sign of resistance.

The reality is that most of us have no clue about our true physical and mental limitations. Quite often, the underlying causes of lapses in discipline are the beliefs we create in our minds that we can't do something. Expecting yourself to be capable, successful, and disciplined will make it all the more likely that you actually are.

Two. Increasing discomfort: "I'd rather not wash the car. It's boring and uncomfortable. I know my spouse asked me to, but it can wait."

Self-discipline is uncomfortable by nature. You would never willingly subject yourself to the struggle of being disciplined unless you had a strong purpose for doing so. The things we willingly do with enjoyment are called *fun*. We never hear about people needing discipline to eat ice cream or play video games.

There's no amount of knowledge, habit formation, thinking, or visualization that will make self-discipline comfortable. It's simply a fact that being disciplined is going to feel like a chore. You're going to hate it at times, even. The key quantity we need more of isn't necessarily always self-discipline itself—it's the amount of discomfort we can handle and tolerate.

This process seeks to turn a stabbing pain into a dull annoyance you can barely feel or a hunger pang that you actually crave because it means you are sticking to your diet. That's as good as it's going to get. Washing the dishes may not morph into something pleasurable, but at least it doesn't have to be an agonizing experience.

Being disciplined comes down to choosing temporary discomfort that helps you in the long-term. Discipline doesn't care if you are exhausted, irritated, or even dejected—that's when you need it the most.

Making a regular habit of embracing uncomfortable situations can have a positive impact on all aspects of your life. Just as lifting weights causes temporary discomfort that allows muscles to grow back stronger, choosing disciplined actions and decision-making also makes your "uncomfortable muscle" stronger.

You don't need to be uncomfortable in your daily life, but being familiar with the feeling sure helps you in the face of actual adversity. You can even create anxiety and uncertainty yourself—so that they are controlled and manageable—to show yourself that you are capable of handling it.

Jia Jiang gave a popular TED Talk about his personal journey outside of his comfort zone, in which he confronted his fear of rejection and the social anxiety that came with it. Jiang wanted to become more confident, so he set out to desensitize himself to rejection by seeking rejection out in some small and controlled way one hundred days in a row. Some of Jiang's rejections included borrowing one hundred dollars from a stranger, requesting a "burger refill," and asking to play soccer in somebody's backyard. When the one hundred days were up, Jiang was a new person with more confidence and a greater appreciation for how kind people are to one another.

Jiang's story of overcoming a fear of rejection is applicable to everybody. Your personal fears and discomforts are also your opportunities to challenge yourself. If you like to be in control, spend a day deferring to other people. If you're more comfortable being passive, spend a day asserting yourself and making more decisions. Whatever you are comfortable doing—do the opposite.

Injecting manageable discomfort and uncertainty into your life isn't difficult to do. You might order the dish on the restaurant menu that has ingredients you haven't heard of before. Or instead of taking a relaxing, hot shower, you could turn the water to cold and force yourself to stand in it until you gain control of your breath and calm your mind. Ask people for discounts that you don't think you'll get. Sit down in a restaurant and then leave after receiving the menu—that walk to the door will feel incredibly long.

Even just doing something spontaneous or out of character can get you out of your comfort zone enough to see that your uncomfortable zone isn't that bad.

As this practice builds your willpower, you can begin to change some of your less beneficial habits. When you feel pulled into a battle with your urges, you'll have the mental strength to resist that temptation and to instead ride the urges out like a wave. And if fear motivates you to avoid your urges altogether by distracting yourself from them, fear is sometimes an opportunity for positive change.

Discomfort and struggle are what make you who you are. You're reading this book because you want to be more self-disciplined, so if you're going to follow through on that, then it's time for you to get comfortable with discomfort.

<u>Three. Excuses for lack of self-discipline to decrease psychological discomfort: "It's perfectly reasonable for me not to wash the car. It's so hot outside I would melt. My spouse didn't really mean it when they asked."</u>

It's time to understand the psychology of excuses a bit better. Making excuses isn't always a deliberate thing. This often makes it hard to pinpoint exactly when we use excuses because we tend toward certain ways of thinking that we just accept as "who we are."

Some of these mindsets are classic personality types that we're all familiar with to an extent. Others are patterns of thought that we don't easily recognize. All of them conspire to make us delay, procrastinate, or simply refuse to do something. But they're also correctable. There are many different mindsets that contribute to the act of excuse-making, but we'll focus on four of the more common ones.

The Perfectionist. This is someone who only acknowledges results if everything goes exactly as they planned. There can be no deviation whatsoever. The Perfectionist takes a stark "all-or-nothing" approach to what they see done: either everything is right or absolutely nothing gets done. And of course, you can bet the standards of a Perfectionist are frequently impossible to meet. They'll have an absolute floor of expectation—if that minimum level of accomplishment isn't meant, the entire project is a waste. So why bother?

How to change the Perfectionist mindset? First, stop thinking of accomplishments as "off/on" switches where there's just the binary of "done/not done." Rather, think of efforts in terms of a "dial" where all efforts are simply measured in levels of intensity. You might be going at eighty-five, fifty percent, or three percent—but you're doing *something* instead of shutting down if things aren't perfectly executed. Something is better than nothing. If you don't come out of the gate stronger than anyone else and do everything perfectly, you can always adjust along the way. It's a fluid process.

The Intimidated. People with this mindset have some commonalities with the Perfectionist in that they use an "ideal condition" to gauge the effectiveness of their efforts. But the Intimidated is more gripped with fear than the Perfectionist. They're afraid they've overshot their ability and have taken on more than they can handle. The Intimidated is driven by a consumptive fear of the unknown and the prospect of total failure. Not only will the results be bad, but they'll also be downright disastrous—the cake in the oven won't just burn; you'll set the entire kitchen on fire.

To tame the Intimidated and overcome your terror of what might happen, the answer's very simple: research. Consider what's the worst-case scenario in your efforts: what would truly define utter catastrophe? Write the answer down and make whatever plans and reinforcements you need to avoid that terrible event from unfolding—and then get to work.

Remember too that failure is something to *learn* from. Just allowing yourself to be defined by failure, without trying to figure out the adjustments you could make to achieve a better result, is a lifelong recipe for eternal procrastination. Resist the urge to overthink and overanalyze in advance and risk "analysis paralysis"—just start something.

The Environment Blamer. People with this mindset are completely at the mercy of their surroundings. They believe they have no input or control about what happens. Life to them is merely a sequence of things that happen to them, not the accomplishments they make. Their belief that outside forces are always conspiring against them leads them to focus only on the external and not at all on their own internal abilities or contributions. This is especially helpful when they're trying to evade responsibility.

To change the environment-blaming mindset, simply accept accountability and realize that things don't have to happen *to you*. Understand that you have just as much ability to affect your surroundings as anyone or anything else. Nothing prevents you from doing so besides yourself. This is a matter of understanding just how much you can participate in your daily life. Question whether the environment is really the cause of your sorrows or whether it's just a convenient excuse. Like the example from earlier, traffic and weather might happen to you, but that doesn't mean you can't account for them yourself.

The Defeatist. This mindset is pessimistic. A Defeatist is certain there's no chance for success—and won't let you forget about it. They've already decided they're not going to succeed, whether they say so or not. The Defeatist uses their lack of optimism to explain their own inabilities—it's not really a reflection of the truth, just that they lack the requisite tools to do anything. More often than not, this attitude stops being an opinion and turns into a self-fulfilling prophecy: they really *will* start stinking at everything.

To change the Defeatist mindset, stop confirming your own failure. Even if it runs counter to your ideas of reality, just attack the problem you're trying to solve or the goal you're trying to achieve. Break the big task down into smaller and more manageable pieces—try to score a few "quick wins" instead of the league championship all at once. It's fair and even prudent to expect hardships or tough stretches, and it's even okay to ask for outside assistance. Just don't declare that failure is inevitable. It's never a done deal.

Excuse-making is the most temporary and fruitless method to feel better. Rather than repair faults and flaws from the ground up, an excuse is more like a Band-Aid that just obscures flaws and does little to fix them. Understanding the nature of excuses helps us see them coming before we speak them. That pause in our thinking can help us see what the *real* situation is and can open up insights into how we can positively affect them. And that leads to a tenacious character that can contend with anything that comes down the path.

Now that we understand the true purpose of excuses and why they are so unhelpful, it's time to learn a method to deal with them as they arise.

The solution isn't necessarily to deny what we're telling ourselves, as that's nearly impossible. Excuses reflect certain states of mind that we may indeed *think* we're experiencing. Instead of denying your excuses, try to dig below the surface and find three components: *the truth, the mentally weak conclusion, and the mentally tough conclusion*. Drawing a clear distinction between these three factors is what will allow you to truly understand your internal dialogue and isolate where you can choose to be tough and resilient.

For example, let's say you have an essay that's due in a few days that will require you to perform research. You have a reasonable window of time to get it completed, but you're exhausted—this is the truth. This is the neutral reality of the situation. This is where the fork in the road appears, and you will make your choice about how to approach it—with toughness or not.

Now ask yourself what an excuse for the truth would sound like. This might be your first impulse—to come up with an excuse *not* to get started. "I could start now, but I'll do much better after I get some sleep." There's your *mentally weak* conclusion: it's allowing you to procrastinate. Even though there might be a hint of truth, its sole purpose is to allow you to take the easy way out. It is indisputably the path of least resistance. It seems to be small and harmless, but it is actually attempting to absolve you of responsibility.

Then ask yourself what the best approach for the truth is. On the other hand, you could say, "I'm tired, but if nothing else, I can do a few small things right now to get the paper going. I could make a rough outline that'll make this paper easier to navigate when I'm more refreshed." That's a *mentally tough* conclusion. It is recognizing what the right and most effective choice is instead of the easy choice. It doesn't demand that you exhaust yourself, but it ensures that you set yourself up for success.

Often, it's only when we engage in this type of role-playing that we can understand we are even making an excuse. You're not required to *reject* the conditions that make up your mentally weak conclusions. No, it's not about becoming a relentless machine in the face of all adversity. Step by step, it's just about realizing that you have many choices and that the choices that lead to toughness are just a slight pivot away. We can move forward only when we realize that excuses are almost always lies.

Four. Avoidance activities to decrease psychological discomfort: "I will clean the bathroom instead. I'm still productive! I'll also arrange my desk. Lots of things getting done today."

Tinkering with your environment can make self-discipline a whole lot easier. If it's *difficult* to distract yourself, then self-discipline might actually become the path of least resistance and you might as well work.

When you study how human behavior evolves over a long time period, environment frequently plays more of a part in success than motivation or skill. Environment is the hidden force that guides human behavior. Yes, incentive, intelligence, and labor are important, but these traits often get overmatched by the surroundings in which we dwell.

External factors are the invisible accomplices for shaping how we react and behave. No matter how self-disciplined we want to be, it is at least partially determined by your physical surroundings.

Brian Wansink of Cornell University conducted a study on dietary habits in 2006 and made an interesting discovery. When people switched from serving plates twelve inches in diameter to plates that were ten inches, they wound up eating twenty-two percent *less* food.

It's an example of how even a minor adjustment in an environment can contribute to an outcome you want. The change in plate size was a minuscule two inches—not quite the width of a smartphone—but yielded more than one-fifth of a decrease in consumption.

Make the easy thing the right thing; make it the default thing, even.

For instance, if you want extra incentive to practice a musical instrument more, you could make a permanent place for the instrument in the middle of a room with instructions of exactly where to pick up. You could also leave a trail of sheet music that literally requires you to pick it up to walk to your bed. If you want to work out more, you're more likely to visit a gym if it's located on your way home from work rather than ten miles in the opposite direction.

You can also put your gym bag in front of your front door, buy a pull-up bar for your kitchen doorway, and only wear shoes that can double as exercise shoes. Finally, if you want to procrastinate less, you can leave reminder Post-Its next to door handles and your wallet (things you will have to touch), leave your work in a place you can't avoid it, and hide your distracting temptations.

Decreasing distraction is a function of *out of sight, out of mind*. For example, supermarkets often place higher-priced items at customers' eye levels to increase the chances they'll buy them. But one could *reverse* this process at home by keeping unhealthy foods away from immediate view and storing them in less visible or harder-to-reach levels. Put your chocolate inside five containers like a Russian nesting doll and put them in a closet. See how often you binge then.

To stop smoking, one might consider removing all the ashtrays from inside the home and placing them as far away as possible on the perimeter of their property so smoking will necessitate a brisk walk in the freezing winter. To keep from sitting down all day, you can switch to a standing desk that will force you to stand up during most working hours. You could also simply remove chairs and coffee tables from the area in which you do most of your work.

Depending on willpower and discipline is risky to say the least, so create an environment that will help you automate your decisions toward self-discipline. In taking that decision out of your hands, you're rewiring yourself to take bad habits out of your routine—and likely saving a little time in the process.

Further Considerations

Set goals. If you Google "goal setting," you get 952 million hits. Setting goals is a much talked about topic. How can setting goals help you break the cycle of lack of self-discipline?

By setting goals, you introduce something external to keep you motivated and accountable. Having an articulated set of goals keeps you on track because you no longer have to convince yourself, "I can do this." Instead, you can say to yourself, "I just need to achieve my goal." The former is easier to let slide, while the latter is more effective because it is tied to a consequence, whether positive or negative.

Another way setting goals can help you break the cycle is by decreasing your discomfort. When your unhelpful assumptions have you feeling uncomfortable, having a clear goal with specific steps may help you put aside some of these feelings and remind you that you everything is proceeding just fine and you don't need to stress or become fearful.

Finally, being able to actively track your progress toward your goal is helpful for adherence. It's motivating. Perhaps you have a log where you document how much water you drink each day. Maybe you mark the length of your run each day on your calendar. Whatever your goal, decide how you are going to monitor your progress toward achieving that goal, because it is going to keep you on track and let you know that your efforts are not in vain. Even just a visual reminder can often be a powerful tool.

When we struggle with self-discipline, we often make the mistake that however we feel is how reality actually is. For instance, because you feel discouraged, you feel that you're destined to fail. Sometimes we need a reminder about what we've accomplished and how far we have come.

All the above benefits of goals are especially true if you attempt to abide by the SMART goal methodology. SMART stands for specific, measurable, attainable, realistic, and with a time frame. Instead of saying that you want to lose weight (too ambiguous and easily shrugged off), you set specific parameters for your goal that help you achieve the goal.

Specific. The goals you set should be precise and unambiguous, otherwise you won't have a clear definition of what you need to accomplish and won't be strongly driven to achieve your aims. The more detail the better. Let's use a common and popular behavioral change as an example of the SMART goals track: establishing a workout routine.

- Why? Because you want to live healthier.

- Who's involved? You, for one. Maybe a personal trainer, too.

- What do you need to accomplish? Building strength and/or losing or gaining weight.

- Which requirements or obstacles do you deal with? You need to establish a routine and use gymnasium equipment. Your obstacles could be personal—self-consciousness in a workout environment or living a bit far from a useful gym facility.

- Where do you need to go to do this? If the gym's too far, maybe there's a space in your house you can clear for working out—or you could just focus on activities you can do anywhere, like running or biking.

These answers don't have to go too far "into the weeds," but they should be clear enough to serve as a statement of purpose and mission.

Measurable. Keeping track of your advancement through your goal is a huge part of remaining motivated. Recording your progress step by step will keep you fully aware of how much you've accomplished and how far you have to go, especially when you're in the latter stages and trying to keep momentum.

For instance, exercise, in particular, thrives on keeping records of your progress: how many reps you do, how many miles you run or bike, by how much you increase your effort over a period of time, how much weight or size you're losing or gaining on a weekly basis, and how far away you are from your targets. If you don't measure it, you won't know it, and you won't do it.

Achievable. Be pragmatic about setting your expectations. Although it's important to stretch your capabilities to grow, your goal should be something you can actually complete. You probably won't rise into a senior executive position if you've only been with a company for six weeks or even six months. Careful estimation of what's realistically possible for you in a modest time frame will help you build your resources gradually and chart your success more surely. If your goal is too easy, you will be bored and unmotivated. If your goal is too difficult, you will become discouraged and quit.

For a workout regimen, results should be achievable according to several factors. Your body build may not support dramatic weight loss or gain, so know what you can expect to achieve, perhaps working from the perspective of getting healthier and changing dietary habits. You're probably going to need to set a workout regimen that fits into your daily schedule and moderate your expectations according to what you can accomplish in that timetable.

Relevant. Do you feel like your goal actually matters? Is it a useful or worthwhile pursuit? Does it fill an established need? Is now the best time to be following this track, or might it be too soon? Is it something that will be valuable in the current personal climate? And are you the best person to bring it to reality?

For the workout example, this isn't a terribly difficult dilemma. Getting healthy is obviously a worthy quest and fills a need. You're of course the best person to make it happen. You could conceivably have a few time-related fixes to think about—there might be a practical reason for you to wait a couple of weeks. Or none at all.

Time-bound. This is a deadline. This could be an additional "when" question in the "specific" category but deserves its own mention. (Plus, we need a "T" section to finish the acronym, anyway.) You need to set a due date or deadline to measure your milestones and keep your focus on the finish line. Of course, this is critical to avoiding procrastination. Set your expectations along a certain time frame. When should you finish the job? What can you do right now, in six months, and in six weeks?

In terms of your workout routine, what size or weight can you expect to be after a certain amount of time (two weeks, six months, a year)? Base your expectations on the other factors in your SMART goal assessment—but once you make a deadline or numeric goal, stick to it.

Olympic athletes only have the opportunity to compete every four years. How can you remain self-disciplined and motivated for so long? The first year might be doable as you are running on enthusiasm, and the fourth year might also be fine as you can run on anticipation. But what about the middle two years? Those are tough times, and setting goals can drastically help your powers of self-discipline.

Time management. Yet another way to help break the cycle of lack of self-discipline is to manage your time better. In general, time management is the ability to get specified things done within the allotted time you have available. It's simple—the worse you are at this skill, the more negativity and discomfort you feel, which leads you down a path of darkness.

A good way to start with time management is to keep a time log. Essentially, you document how you spend each minute of your day for at least a week. This can be done on paper, on a calendar or e-calendar, in a spreadsheet, or whatever way works best for you. Whatever method you choose, be brutally honest about your time. This will provide the most information and help you on your quest to become a better time manager.

At the end of the week, you can look back and see not only what you accomplished, but you can also look for trends. Look for the time of day that you are most productive. Moving forward, you may want to schedule your most important tasks of the day in that time frame. Maybe your time log is an eye-opening look at just how much time you waste. How much time do you spend on social media, surfing the Internet, etc.? If you've really been authentic in recording how you spend your time, it can be a truly valuable tool.

Time management can actually help break the cycle at almost any point. If your unhelpful assumption is fear of the unknown, time management can help by creating routines and systems that allow you to have a better handle on what's coming next in your day, month, etc.

If you are feeling uncomfortable—say, anxious or frustrated—a good time management system can help you stay or get back on track and alleviate some of those feelings of discomfort by giving you a framework in which to operate.

Time management also helps when you are making excuses. It's harder to make an excuse when you have something scheduled on your calendar. By having an appointment on your calendar, you know there's a deadline, and that creates a sense of urgency, thereby spurring you into action rather than encouraging you to come up with excuses. After all, many of us claim to work better under a time constraint, so you can test this theory on yourself through better time management.

If you are in avoidance mode? When you are avoiding a task, you are typically replacing it with something of low or lower priority. By honing your time management skills, you can better schedule time for your priority tasks, but you can also schedule your "time killers" or down times. By scheduling both, it helps keep you on task for the more important things since you know you have time scheduled to do other things.

Finally, time management can be beneficial when it comes to consequences. You may be able to avoid some of the negative consequences by being an effective time manager. By scheduling your time, you will be less likely to fall behind, which can create stressful demands on you and your time. You are also likely to avoid failing at a task because you've planned things out ahead of time.

Takeaways:

- It can be tempting to think of your self-discipline as isolated incidents that you must overcome. This would be a mistake. Self-discipline does not exist in a vacuum and is highly dependent on five factors that make up the cycle of self-discipline. Or, more accurately, the cycle of *laziness*.
- The phases are unhelpful assumptions ("Life is short, so I should enjoy it and not spend my precious time washing that dusty car!"); increasing discomfort from knowingly avoiding responsibility ("I'd rather not wash the car. It's boring and uncomfortable."); excuses to

decrease discomfort ("It's perfectly reasonable for me not to wash the car. It's so hot outside I would melt."); avoidance activities to decrease discomfort ("I will clean the bathroom instead. I'm still productive!"); and negative and positive consequences from avoiding responsibility ("Ah, I feel better about myself now. Oh, wait. I still need to wash that car . . .")—at which point you find yourself right back at the beginning, except with less willpower and incentive than before because negative consequences create pessimism, while positive consequences create self-sabotage.

- Aside from knowledge of the cycle and what you tend to fall prey to, there are specific ways to deal with four of the five phases of the cycle. Regarding unhelpful assumptions, instead embody the empowering belief of the forty percent rule. Regarding discomfort, change your expectations and actively practice discomfort to build your mental toughness. Regarding excuses, learn how to reframe your excuses and stop falling into the common traps and self-lies. Regarding avoidance activities, it's a matter of out of sight, out of mind; if you cannot find distractions, you cannot avoid.

- Other general considerations for beating the cycle of lacking self-discipline are creating goals to reduce discomfort and improve time management, and developing skills to stop making excuses so frequently. Beat the cycle!

Chapter 3. Yes or No?

To build self-discipline, one needs to self-monitor. At some point, you need to be able to know that what you're doing is wrong—this moment of realization will probably be after the fact, but you might even catch yourself in the middle of it from time to time. All the self-discipline in the world isn't useful if you don't know when you need to exercise it—either in the present moment or in the future.

It's about making that switch from unconscious into conscious. From acting automatically to acting with deliberate purpose. And it all starts with being able to honestly look at what we're doing.

Unfortunately, most types of self-analysis are completely foreign to us. It runs counter to how we are wired because it involves stepping outside of our self-interested tendencies. Thus, it's not a skill we practice, and this leads to us often being unable to explain why we do what we do. We do, we react, and then the conscious thought comes after—if at all. Frankly, we walk around day to day with such a lack of self-awareness that we can barely recite the steps of our work commute.

As bothersome and painful as self-analysis is, flat-out *ignoring* or not knowing yourself is not an acceptable alternative. You're not going to get far with willful ignorance or lack of perspective. You will have to be tough on yourself and ask yourself some hard questions.

That's what this chapter is about. It contains questions you can ask yourself whenever you come to a stopping point or a fork in the road in your progress, especially if you sense you might give up and drift off into idleness, sloth, or undisciplined thinking. You can (and should) ask yourself these questions whenever you have time to do a mental "check-in."

There is, however, one very important facet about these questions: your answers to most of them—no matter what the situation at the time you ask—must be either yes or no. No gray areas, no "but," no "it depends," and no "I don't know." Just yes or no. No explanations allowed. One-word answers only.

It may sound like I'm encouraging you to set up a false dichotomy: a situation where you're forced into choosing one of only two acceptable answers when in reality the situation may be much more complex. This might put you into a conundrum when you can't clearly answer yes or no. But you're right. That's exactly what I'm doing.

Here's why. First, a drawn-out answer can get in the way of executing action or change. Giving a complex answer to any of these questions could lead you down a rabbit hole of overthinking, which will likely delay action on your part. This is otherwise known as *analysis paralysis*. This is also a slippery slope to creating excuses, which we already know are no good.

Second and more importantly, just answering yes or no to these questions—all of which, I'm sure, *can* be answered more deeply and thoroughly—forces you to either state a harsh truth about yourself or know that you need to take action. When you have no option to equivocate, justify, or overexplain, you're forced to make a sharp, clear judgment on yourself. If you are over fifty percent at any point toward yes or no, that's your answer. Your justifications, defenses, or explanations about why you're doing or not doing it don't matter. Either you're doing something or you're not. And most of the time when you're forced to answer like this, you're not going to like what you find. This pushes you act.

Were you late to baseball practice?

Well, there was so much traffic and you guys didn't start on time anyway. This might be true, but that's not the question that was asked. Instead, this answer provides no information and displays a similar amount of self-awareness. You can almost feel the attempt to wriggle out of responsibility in this response. This person doesn't think they are the type to be late to baseball practice. You are haring their attempts to minimize psychological tension in themselves.

Yes. Now you've reached a harsh truth. You can either choose to accept that your actions define you, or you can exercise better discipline in the future to change this answer. This ends up being an important piece of the puzzle with the yes/no questions we use.

Importantly, you haven't changed anything—the truth was always the same (you were, in fact, late)—only now you are acknowledging it. Now you are looking at the fact without any excuses or justifications to cushion it.

The entire crux of self-discipline is that you are doing what you need to do, despite wanting to give up and despite pain and discomfort. Thus, it is only appropriate that you stop the habit of justifications and equivocations and simply get things done, no matter how valid those excuses might be. That's why you bought this book, after all.

I know it's also true that there were roadblocks and the practice started late anyway, but can you see how none of this actually matters? You can discuss all the mitigating factors, roadblocks, issues, or complications when you're in the post-mortem phase—when your projects are done and submitted. Do first and stop talking in circles.

With that, let's dive in. When you feel you're at a crossroads or a stopping point in getting to where you want to be, the questions you need to ask are as follows. It might help to jot them on a notecard somewhere or even carry them with you as a sort of self-discipline compass whenever needed.

1. Will this course of action create a gap between my ideal self and my non-desired self?

You want the answer here to be no—and you should do everything possible to not answer yes. Your ideal self is the one who possesses the self-discipline of a Shaolin monk on steroids.

One more thing: you have to be honest. Really honest. Give yourself credit for being a master liar—to yourself that is. Be on razor-sharp alert for any temptation to tell yourself that the desired self is really closer than it looks, or that the gap is not really serious, and so on.

Let's say you're striving to be more productive at work. You fear that a lot of your colleagues have no idea why you're at work—you're nice enough, but they can't name one thing that you've done to make yourself indispensable. You become aware of this possibility and it frightens you. You start to see *yourself* that way.

The thing is, you don't feel like yourself at work. You're riddled with anxiety and never really feel like people know who you are. You don't have this issue in your social life. In fact, when explaining it to others, you give yourself an alter ego to show how you're almost a different person entirely when you're at the office—it's called "Rain."

Rain is easily distracted. They spend a lot of time online at work, not always in work-related pursuits. They don't have a huge attention span at meetings. They do exactly the minimum required to not get fired. But given enough time, Rain's lack of ambition and effort will make them redundant or expendable.

But the person who you want to be is named, somewhat audaciously, "Steel." Steel is constantly assured. They never lack confidence. They know everything that goes on in their work. They don't have a lot of time for distraction. If there's a moment Steel's not working, they're probably doing research on a future project or idea. They're optimistic and charming. They have a lot of answers (though they'll say, "I don't have all the answers," without sounding desperate). And of course, their work ethic is second to none and they have the self-discipline of a Buddhist monk on a three-month silent retreat.

Your conflict here is between the idea of your *ideal* self—Steel, the kind of person who reflects your highest values, standards, and capabilities—and your *undesired* self—Rain, the role you might indulge in sometimes but strive to avoid as much as possible.

Will your actions bring you closer to Steel or Rain? Will you move further away from your ideal, or will you grow closer to achieving it?

Again, this is a yes/no question. "There may be a slight gap, but down the line it might be worth it," or, "Well, you see, this time is different because . . ." are not acceptable answers. "Yes, the gap is bigger," or, "No, the gap is not bigger," are your only choices. Don't give excuses or justifications any room to wriggle in.

This question is important to ask is because it raises the absolutely frightening possibility that you are actually not the type of person you want to be and that your identity is at risk. It raises the possibility that you are lying to yourself; it creates a conflict between your words and your actions. It gives direct consequences to your actions by linking you to either Steel or Rain.

Thus, you are pushed to protect your self-worth and image. The verbal realization of, "Yes, I'm not who I want to be, am supposed to, or pride myself on being," just might shake you into action to do something about it. It should inspire you to make the first efforts to instill the discipline that will get you toward your ideal self. Here, instead of being overwhelmed by psychological tension and avoiding it, you are using to shine a light on precisely those things that are not working for you.

This question tends to feel a little confrontational, so here is an alternative phrasing: *"Does this course of action get me closer to my goal?"* Some people are simply more goal-oriented than identity-driven. It's easier for them to measure their progress by the attainment of milestones or targets rather than in terms of self-worth. In the end, this version of the yes/no question also links direct consequences to your actions.

No matter which iteration of the question you ask yourself, it should make you consider cold reality. Are you truly acting in your own best interests and bringing yourself closer to your ideal? Or are you working against your benefit? If you come to the conclusion that you're not serving your self-interest, then what exactly are you getting out of this deal? Will it be worth the sacrifice? At least gain self-awareness that you are making a trade-off.

2. Does this action truly represent my intentions?

Hopefully you answer yes, because self-discipline is reflected only when actions and intentions match. If not, what are your actions actually working toward?

Let's say you have a goal of writing a novel. You think about it a lot. When you're working your day job, chipping away at another responsibility you need to look after, you're still imagining yourself as a published author—or at least somebody who's written a complete book. You're planning characters and plot points in your head and seemingly dreaming about your work all the time.

When you get free time after work or on the weekends, you're doing a lot to unwind: hitting the coffee shop, taking long walks, meeting friends for lunch, spending time online, hitting the bars at night, basic distractions. You might be talking about your book to friends, who at least appear to be interested.

The one thing you're *not* doing, though, is actually working on the book. You're not committing anything to writing. You've got an empty file folder on your desktop, waiting to be filled with sketches, ideas, and text, but there's nothing in it.

You're not doing anything *wrong*, necessarily—but are your actions actually accomplishing what you want? Are you actively working toward finishing that novel and trying to get on the road to be a full-time writer?

That's the next line of interrogation for you: are your activities in alignment with your intentions? Is what you mentally desire being translated into action? Are you doing what you need to be doing, or are you merely paying it lip service? Even worse, has your attention drifted away from your best intentions, leading you to act without a goal at all? The easiest example of this would be sending work emails on your phone but getting sidetracked by social media.

You probably don't have any problem imagining or even meditating on your desires. You may have a very clear picture in your head as to what you want to be. But unless you're actually gearing your efforts toward fulfilling that goal, those thoughts and intentions don't mean a thing.

You won't get credit, acclaim, or congratulations for *thinking* a good game— you get them for *doing* something. You can have very articulated, very clear visions for what you want to be, but if what you're doing isn't directly contributing to those intentions, you're not getting anywhere. Intentions don't pay the bills; for instance, don't pat yourself on the back for *thinking* about bringing your significant other a present—this won't be very convincing to them.

The answer to this question has ramifications outside the attainment of your goals: it also strikes to the heart of your character. Someone who talks a good game but can't match it with definitive actions could be considered undependable or untrustworthy.

Your reputation hinges on what you're actually able to accomplish. Not being able to match your ambitions with actual work is a sign of mental frailty, no matter how complete your idea might be in your head. Anyone can talk like a writer, and it might be good for a lively evening of interesting discussion. But that completely evaporates when the conversation's over if you don't actually *work* on the novel. Words and evocative speech ultimately don't mean anything—action does.

That's why this question is important. And like the first question, it might be more helpful if your answer is no—again, without any conditions, explanations, footnotes, or excuses. Just no. Hopefully the cold shock of that no will spur you to put your intentions into actions.

This question could be asked about almost any aspect of your life. "Am I being a responsible parent and keeping my behavior in line with what I tell my kids?" "Am I working hard enough to reach my goal of learning a new language?" "Am I really working hard enough at being the best pool player in the western hemisphere, or do I need to spend more time practicing my bank shots?" Any kind of ambition or goal that you have in mind, no matter how personal or public, is easily addressed by asking yourself if your actions are meeting your intentions.

Yes or no. That's almost always enough to get you moving in the right direction. If not, it will be because of your intentions themselves, not how self-disciplined you are.

3. Am I merely uncomfortable?

Discomfort is a funny thing. We all do our best to avoid it, and most of us attempt some form of personal development precisely because we want lives with *less* discomfort and more serenity, ease and enjoyment. This goes back to the assumption that we shouldn't suffer, ever, and if we do, we should act in whatever way is necessary to end it. We think: this discomfort is unbearable. I hate it and want it to stop. Something is wrong.

But is it?

Is your reason for not wanting to exercise self-discipline related only to mere discomfort and nothing actually harmful? You want to answer no here; otherwise, you are admitting that you melt faster than an ice cube in summer. Consequently, you may realize how much you disempower yourself.

Let's talk about going to the neighborhood gym. Almost anybody who's in decent physical shape, it stands to reason, has probably conquered most of their self-consciousness about working out in public and has no problem sweating it out in the presence of strangers.

For those who *aren't* top physical specimens, the story can be quite different. Exercising can make them uncomfortable for a myriad of reasons. From the moment they get on a treadmill, they may feel like they're being watched and judged. If they try to do an arm curl, they may feel embarrassed or timid in the presence of someone who's obviously done thousands of them. If they're trying to work off the paunch around their stomach, they may feel that other people are watching and appraising them harshly. This is of course ignoring the muscular fatigue and soreness that can follow.

Thus, for someone who is debating going to the gym, is mere discomfort holding them back, or is it the prospect of real harm? That's the crux of the third yes/no question: "Do I not want to do this just because it makes me feel uncomfortable? Or is this actually having a negative, harmful effect on me?"

I'm willing to bet that ninety-nine times out of one hundred, the answer is yes—it's merely uncomfortable. You are being pushed out of your comfort zone. You will suffer a bit mentally. Your body will grow sweaty and fatigued. Your brain will be exercised to its full capacity. You may experience some negative emotions, such as stress and anxiety. You will recover just fine without lasting repercussions. This is all discomfort.

And then?

And then nothing. So are you the type of person to pack it in just because you're uncomfortable? Feel free to slide down the slippery slope of what kind of person that might make you. Your worst-case scenarios and wild justifications are just providing a flimsy reason to avoid discomfort. In fact, they're nothing more than mental illusions. This question forces you to face the shame that you are easily stopped by discomfort— discomfort has and never will be a legitimate reason to not exercise self-discipline. And thus, this shame should propel you into action. This is a question where the yes/no dichotomy is particularly effective.

Every single thing we do to better ourselves, to effect positive change in our lives, is going to involve some measure of inconvenience, discomfort, or fatigue, at least in the beginning. It might even involve minor pain, especially if you're working out for the first time.

But are any of those consequences inherently *harmful*? Do they really undermine our integrity, threaten our health, compromise our sanity? No, they don't. There are a thousand clichés that reflect that truth, like "no pain, no gain." Effecting real change in your life is going to involve a measure of discomfort. I can't think of any kind of emotional, physical, spiritual, or occupational change that doesn't entail some irritation, soreness, inconvenience, or bother. If they didn't, everybody would do it.

Think about this question with everything you do that's causing you some measure of discomfort: you have the choice to be lazy and weak-spirited or get into action.

4. What would I do if I had no choice but to exercise self-discipline?

We'll break from the theme of the chapter here for a moment, as this isn't a yes/no question. Sorry, I couldn't resist. Still, keep the answer short and sweet and rooted in reality without rationalizations.

Let's for a moment pretend that you don't have the option to choose the right path, but that the right path is nonnegotiable. If there was a gun pointed at your head, what would happen if you were forced to exercise self-discipline? You might be forced to admit that *absolutely nothing* bad would happen, and in fact, you'd be better positioned than before. Similar to the last question, you may experience discomfort, but you'd get through it and persevere.

Let's go back to the gym. You've been working out for an hour. You've just received a phone call that if your heartbeat drops below a certain rate, your entire family will die. So you jump on the treadmill and try to hold on for dear life. Nothing feels comfortable at this point, as you have fatigue, self-consciousness, revulsion at your own body odor, sweat marks everywhere, the whole nine yards. Your lungs are burning and your mouth is dry.

Miraculously, this criminal is caught after an hour. Besides those discomforts, what awful consequences have come as a result of your being forced to work out?

None. The point is to understand that the worst-case scenarios we dream up will never occur, the benefits of your efforts are going to be real, and the price you have to pay to get them, in the end, won't be much at all. You come out the other end of the action you focused on and you're still alive. You might not even remember the pain or discomfort later. If you do, you'll probably firmly believe it was worth all the pain to get where you wanted to go. When you force yourself into something, you have nothing to lose but everything to gain.

When you try to summon up the will to exercise self-discipline, picture yourself as having no Plan B whatsoever. Don't look for shortcuts, don't search for less taxing or exhausting schemes, and don't try to negotiate with yourself. Don't even begin to think about the possibility of an alternative. Again, gun to your head, you'd sigh, groan a bit, and then set to your task without any other consequences. Imaginary crisis averted.

Hopefully, it will make you understand how your fleeting impulses of annoyance or minor discomfort can derail you from your plans—and how they shouldn't. When you emerge from the other side of the task you felt was insurmountable, you give yourself the chance to say, "Oh. That wasn't actually so bad." The satisfaction you receive from your positive consequences will be more than enough to strike those small peeves from your memory.

5. Is "I don't want to" a good enough excuse to not do something?

You already know the answer to this question—no. And hopefully, the way it is phrased makes you realize that "I don't want to" is a bit of an entitled and lazy thing to say. And you don't want to be entitled and lazy, do you? No matter how you dress it up or rationalize it, most of the time, we just don't want to exercise discipline because *we don't want to.*

We can play devil's advocate first, to bring some context to this question.

Why should you do something you really don't want to do? Life is a complicated enough affair as it is. Why weigh it down even more with something that you just don't want to experience or put effort toward things that make you miserable to any degree, even if they will result in positive consequences? What's the difference? Don't you have free will? What about living for *carpe diem* and truly living life because you're only young once?

Those are all true. But now imagine people who do *not* have your range of options.

Some people have to do things that nobody else wants to do to make ends meet. They work menial or strenuous jobs or work multiple jobs because they absolutely have to. Some of them have to take care of entire families, which might restrict them from things they really want to do. In fact, they may be so busy or preoccupied that they don't have time to even *think* about what they really want to do. They have no time for anything except working, eating, and sleeping. They indeed have the proverbial gun to their head from the previous question. And then they have to do that every day of the week.

Some of them may be perfectly content with this—maybe they find meaning in what they do, and that's enough for them. That is respectable.

You, however, by virtue of being able to hem and haw and procrastinate, are in a position of privilege to have the choices they don't. The chores and tasks you have to endure to get to the goal you want to reach are opportunities they do not have. They'd love to have the time to learn a foreign language, develop a knowledgeable appreciation for art, or spend time learning to communicate with their loved ones. They'd also love the choice to not do something they need to do. They just don't have the ability or time. You do.

And not to be mean, but let's be honest: if a longshoreman heard you complaining about the leg cramps you got while doing sit-ups, he might think you're being a little, well, *ridiculous*. He has no choice but to wake up at 5:00 a.m. each day and work until 8:00 p.m. How's that for a bit of perspective? Surely you can push a bit harder in the gym. Surely you can make the bed every morning. Surely that darned car can finally get washed.

The answer to this question, then, is hopefully no, it's not a good excuse for anything. Everybody does something they don't want to do from time to time, but some people don't have the opportunity to do anything else. Turn that realization into a sense of gratitude that you *can* do it. That's not just "the right way" to be, either: it will give you a positive outlook, because it's impossible to feel gratitude and negativity at the same time.

Spend some time thinking about people who *have* to do those arduous or dreadful jobs every day of their lives—write them down in a list if you have to. Then put yourself in proper perspective about the pesky discomforts or chores you have to do to get to your goal. Your being able to do those annoying things is actually a great *freedom*.

These things you want to avoid are only drudgery if you choose to see them that way. Coming at a task from a mindset of gratitude versus dread will create vastly different outcomes. In the grand scheme of things, you're not asking all that much of yourself, and the end result will be far more worthy of your mental energy than what you spend to complain about them.

6. Am I doing the *right* thing or the *easy* thing?

Sorry—another deviation from the theme of the chapter. Yet it's still a helpful question to bring clarity to what you're trying to accomplish at the moment or in the future.

Going to the gym would be the right thing, while the easy thing would be staying at home. The easy thing would also be researching healthy recipes online or anything else you do to slightly ease your guilt. Unfortunately, doing the right thing usually means doing the hard thing.

Actually, they are almost always the exact same thing. The average person doesn't typically choose things that are difficult when there is an alternative, which is why self-discipline is often the missing component for many people who don't fulfill their goals. People drift toward the path of least resistance, consciously or not. If you don't want that to be you, you'll need to be able to consciously answer whether you are doing *that*—or doing what's *right*.

When you can't confidently say that you're doing the right thing, you're not—and then you are forced to compare the difference between right and easy. If you're not doing what you should be, then anything else out of your mouth is an excuse, plain and simple.

Instead of beating around the bush and soothing your ego, it would actually be better to start being honest and upfront with yourself about your behavior. Categorize your actions into right or easy.

Running to lose weight: right thing. Skipping a workout: easy thing. Cutting workout short: easy thing.

Instead of rationalizing skipping a run because "it's too hot outside" or "it's too late," you would just start saying, "I'm not going to run today because I'm too soft and lazy to maintain discipline."

In reality, why are you skipping the run? Because you're lazy. You know the right thing to do is run. Therefore, you are taking the easy way out. In effect, you become brutally honest and confrontational with yourself, which is sometimes the only way to get a message across.

You should always want to answer that you're doing what's right, and that will frequently mean that you have to make a little extra effort. But when you do it consistently, that extra effort pays off.

For example, you might have the opportunity to cheat while taking an exam. Knowing that they wouldn't be caught, the typical student probably takes that opportunity to cheat and runs with it. But then the final exam comes around, and now the test-taking environment is much more closely monitored to the point that cheating would be risky or even impossible. The students who didn't cheat on previous exams and relied on their own studying will have actually learned the material throughout the semester and given themselves a good shot at success, while the students who cheated their way through the entire semester won't know anything on the final exam.

Reaching your goals isn't all that different from succeeding on that final exam. Sure, you might find little successes from shortcuts from rationalizations along the way, but eventually it catches up to you, and you'll find you don't have what it takes. Doing the right thing may feel like the harder route in the moment, but when you do it consistently, it winds up being the most efficient route to accomplishing your goals.

Is there a *real* obstacle to my goal that can't be overcome?

Think of this question as an excuse-buster. An excuse is something that appears on the surface to be quite rational but, in reality, is nothing more than an attempt to wriggle out of something that is difficult or uncomfortable—or even just something that takes you slightly out of your comfort zone.

Look, obviously on occasion there really will be a good reason for you not to do your workout that day (Both of your arms have suddenly fallen off?), but usually there's a work around no matter what (looks like it's a leg day, then!). The truth is that most of the reasons we give ourselves for not doing something are bogus, and deep down, we know it.

What is really the obstacle?

Think about it—a person who truly doesn't want to do something won't do it, no matter how easy it is for them. They'll dream up any number of excuses to say why they can't. And a person who truly does want to do something cannot be dissuaded, i.e. no matter what obstacles emerge, they do what they want to do.

What this means is that it's not even really about the "obstacles" at all. It's about our will, intention and self-discipline. If you catch yourself telling yourself a nice little story about why you couldn't possibly do the thing you said you were going to do, stop, take a close look at what's going on, and ask, is there *really* an obstacle in the way here? Or is my attitude the obstacle?

Another way to look at it—there may be obstacles, sure, but then again, there always are. There are so many obstacles in life you may as well say there are none, because to have something standing in your way is pretty much the norm. It'll always be something—the weather, money, other people being idiots, tiredness, work, you name it. If not one thing, then the other.

But are those obstacles *that cannot be overcome*? Probably not.

Either you can a) acknowledge that you're just making excuses and refuse to believe them, or b) you can take the obstacle at face value, but refuse to let it mean anything, i.e. sure it's going to be tricky, but so what? You'll just find another way. If we're honest, the answer to this question is almost always "nope."

What is the outcome of this action if I continue along this path?

The easy, tempting, distracting thing is right here in front of you, promising instant gratification. Indulging conceals its true cost, though, which only kicks in later down the line, in the future. Is your present self-engaging in behavior that's screwing over your future self? In other words, are you doing things that your future self will regret?

The idea behind this question is to activate long-term thinking and downplay our tendency to focus only on the immediate rewards of an action in the present. Here are two options:

Option A: Pleasure and ease.
Option B: Turning down pleasure and ease.

The choice is an easy one, right? You go with A. Life is hard, why not make the best of it? Take the afternoon off for no reason, have a "treat" or do a sloppy job on a task just to get it done. But look at this set of options:

Option A: Pleasure and ease, followed by guilt and shame (at ten minutes) then regret (at ten days) a deep sense of disappointment in yourself (ten weeks) and then the feeling that your dreams have passed you by and it's too late to do anything now (ten months or years).
Option B: Turning down pleasure and ease, followed by nothing in particular (ten

minutes) but then a little pride at having strength to be self-disciplined (ten days) a stronger sense of focus (ten weeks) and the completion of your dream goal (ten months or years).

Which seems like the better choice now? They are, of course, both the same options in each case, only the second pair truly accounts for the *consequences* of your actions, and takes a long term view. The trouble is that all the less-beneficial actions seem to have rewards that play out instantly with a bill that comes later, whereas the better choices take time for their benefits to show. If we aren't patient, focused, and diligent, we will always pick option A . . . but still pay for it later. The old adage "act in haste, repent at leisure" captures this idea somewhat.

Actions mature. Sometimes, results only fully appear long after their instigating action. By asking the above question, though, you're correcting this bias for rewards in the present and doing a full accounting of what an action really costs you. Don't choose something simply according to the benefits you perceive in the moment. When you choose something, you are also choosing the consequences of that thing, even consequences that play out over *decades*; you are choosing what happens over the next minutes, days, years, months. Also ask if you did this action, what other actions would it make easier and more probable in future—and are those what you really want? In other words, the more choose pleasure and ease, the easier it is to keep on choosing it.

The next time you are faced with something that threatens to derail your disciplined action, ask what indulging looks like down the line. Look at possible outcomes and consequences. Ask what happens in ten minutes, ten days, ten weeks, ten years. Hey, there's a chance that acting now has few if any consequences, and it's best to seize the day and have a good time. But at least choose that option with open eyes.

Takeaways:

- Yes or no? Just a simple answer, please, with no BS. This chapter is all about self-interrogation and digging into your excuses and rationalizations to avoid exercising self-discipline. What follows is typically self-awareness at how casually you view avoiding work. There are six questions to bring clarity. Most are indeed yes/no questions to force you to either admit a harsh truth or take action.

- Will this course of action create a gap between my ideal self and my non-desired self? Alternatively, does this action take me closer or farther from my goals?
- Does this action truly represent my intentions? If not, then what the heck am I doing?
- Am I merely uncomfortable? Am I letting mere discomfort keep me from my goals? Am I so mentally weak?
- What would I do if I had no choice but to exercise self-discipline? Certainly *not* the worst-case scenario.
- Is "I don't want to" a good enough excuse to not do something? You may have the ability to use this excuse, but what about those who are never able to take a break and *have to act* every single time? It's difficult to feel gratitude and lack self-discipline at the same time.

- Am I doing the *right* thing or the *easy* thing? There's usually only one path to what you want, and it's not typically an easy one.
- Is there a *real* obstacle to my goal that I can't overcome? This focuses you on the fact that most of the time, the so-called obstacle is not the problem, but our attitude is. If we wanted to do it, no obstacle would stop us, and if we didn't want to do it, we wouldn't, even if there we zero obstacles.
- What is the outcome of this action if I continue along this path? Switch your focus away from instant gratification and see how a decision plays out over time, from ten minutes to ten years into the future. When you choose something, you are also choosing the consequences of that thing, even if those consequences don't kick in for a while.

Chapter 4. The Neuropsychology of Self-Discipline

Understanding how your brain might naturally work against you, and building smart habits to counteract that cycle is super important when it comes to self-discipline. But in this chapter, we'll be taking a look at a few extra, last-resort resources and small things you can do in everyday life to give you the best chance at actually achieving the important goals you set for yourself.

Figure Out Where You Are

Imagine a perfectly self-motivated and disciplined person. What do they look like? What is their attitude to life and how do they conduct themselves?

There's a reason people respond well to inspiration al figures and motivational speakers—their lives can act as a blueprint for a more productive and self-controlled life. They're like models that pave the way, showing us how it's done (or at least, one way it could be done!).

Usually, these people are not that dissimilar from one another. They seem to share a handful of traits and personal characteristics that are fundamental to their success. It follows that if we want to act and behave more like them, then we can start by developing those characteristics in ourselves. That is, it's a question of not what to do, but how to be.

The following characteristics signal a disciplined high-achiever in any area of life, and are essential for succeeding at any chosen goal.

Strong sense of purpose – The big WHY behind everything you do. Without the fire of purpose, calling or passion behind you, you're not truly motivated. To be highly effective and disciplined, your purpose has to be genuine, clear, and come from within.

Seeks out positive mentors – Your role models matter. If they don't have inspirational people around them, the self-disciplined seek them out, deliberately valuing their support, input and guidance. They are not jealous or threatened but inspired by others' success.

Sensory rich vision – People with the discipline to succeed see a vision of their goal—they literally see it. And smell it, hear it, almost *taste* it. They entertain visions of their own success, rather than dwelling in detail on ideas of their failure. They fill their minds not just with powerful positive imagery, but with positive material on all their five senses. Their visionary goal is imagined in 3D.

Strong belief in self – Those who put their willpower to work bringing their dreams to life must, at a fundamental level, believe that it's actually possible, and that they have it in them to do what it takes. This may mean self-belief even when nobody else can support your vision. Crippling self-doubt and low self-esteem, on the other hand, will only interfere with your self-discipline.

Ability to plan and organize – Of course, it's not just vision and self-confidence. People who can get things done are those that *plan* to get things done. They know how to plot a course of action and they know how to coordinate and focus their efforts to achieve that. Chaos and disorganization can dissipate your energies and waste your time.

High value on education, learning, and skills – For some, education is an obligation, or at bets a means to an end. But for high achievers, learning is a way of life, and they relish the chance to develop, to correct misunderstandings, and to challenge themselves to go further.

Patient perseverance – To find effort and motivation in yourself is one thing, but can you sustain that level for a prolonged period? Can you wake up day after day and keep going, even in the face of intermittent or delayed rewards? Self-discipline requires enough patience to wait for the results of your actions to bear fruit, and to keep consistent throughout. Without this trait, we give up easily and quit things when they don't work out exactly as we want first time round, or we look for quick fixes and hacks rather than putting in the work.

Seeing work as pleasure and play – People who achieve well at their work usually have a mindset where work is not work, but something enjoyable, interesting, engrossing. They don't resent it or find it boring. In fact, they may have very little distinction between "work" and "play." This attitude means that they act from curiosity and inner drives, rather than feeling it's a burden placed on them.

So, how do you fare on each of these traits?

Time for a little self-reflection. You can conduct a mini appraisal of yourself any time you like, to get a good idea of your weak spots, but also to take note where you're improving. When you know what areas need attention, you can plan your progress a little more carefully.

Try this: on each of the following eight characteristics, rate yourself on a scale of one to ten where one is the lowest or most negative end of the continuum, and ten the highest.

Sense of purpose
Positive mentors
Sensory-rich vision
Self-belief
Planning and organization
Education and skills
Patient perseverance
Seeing work as play

You can add up your scores for each characteristic for a global score and then compare this in time, or you could do a few self-assessments over the course of a few weeks or months to see how you're developing in any one area.

Naturally, doing a self-assessment is just a snapshot. It takes real honesty, and it's not enough on its own—you need to take what insights you glean from it and actually make proactive changes. It may feel a little silly at first, but if you can concretely see the improvement in an area, in numbers, you may feel more empowered and confident in the steps you're taking to be more disciplined.

Similarly, if you're trying a new technique or method and after three months' notice no improvement, you can safely conclude that it's not right for you, knowing that your decision is honest and data-driven, rather than just being procrastination or an excuse.

Bringing Self-Discipline Traits to Life

Let's look in more detail at how we can actually develop some of these traits in ourselves. There are practical ways to improve in each dimension, or all of them, and often improvement in one will spur and support improvement in another. For our purposes, let's say that our main goal is to *create motivation and inspiration*. We want to spark and grow that passion, energy and even obsession required to build our dreams and get to work on what we care about.

Motivation and inspiration are emotional reactions, but they are also a result of the traits discussed above. If we are deficient in any of them, there'll be a corresponding weakening in our overall sense of energy and motivation. So, being fired up with passion and purpose is not something we can *directly* cause in ourselves. However, we can *indirectly* create the right conditions in which our passion can ignite—and we can do it with conscious creation and self-discipline, one action at a time. Let's take a look at the eight traits again and a few tips and tricks for developing each within yourself.

Sense of Purpose

The tricky thing with this is that nobody can tell you what feels meaningful or worthwhile to you. It really has to come from within. Many people embark on what they think is a self-discipline program, but in reality, they have merely substituted the teacher or facilitator's vision for their own, assuming that they want the same things that they do.

To strengthen your sense of purpose, you need one thing: self-knowledge.

You need to know with honesty and clarity who you are, what makes you tick what values matter (and which ones don't matter!) and what ultimately drives you. Bear in mind, though, that this can change with time. What felt like our life purpose at fifteen may not feel that way at thirty-five. That's why we need to constantly reappraise so that we can fine tune and readjust, making sure our goals are OUR goals and align with us as individuals.

Therapy always helps with self-discovery, but there are some easy ways to remind yourself of what your purpose is. Ask yourself:

- If you suddenly won the lottery, what would you do? What does your answer say about what you ultimately value in life?
- What would you like your obituary to say about you?
- In the past, when you've been fiercely motivated to work on something, what was driving you?
- Who do you admire most, and what about them speaks to you? Is anything of them in you, too?

- Which activities most allow you to get into a "flow"?

Once you've identified your values, purposes, and deeper guiding principles, write them down somewhere. These are like your compass to guide you back home when you're lost and floundering.

Positive Mentors

Let's be honest, not everyone is blessed with good role models. In fact, most of us are likely surrounded by those who have been modeling passive, negative behaviors to us all our lives, or else we find ourselves in situations where we are unable to develop into our full potential.

Luckily, we can choose. If you rated yourself quite low on this characteristic, take heart that there is a lot you can do to invite quality people into your world. There is a saying that you eventually resemble the five people you most spend time with. Whether this is true or not, there's no doubt that our sense of identity, our habits and our mindsets are powerfully influenced by those around us. Here's a two-step activity to try and raise your score in this area.

Firstly, try to identify anyone who is actively holding you back. You know the kinds of people—pessimistic, critical, sabotaging, or just plain mean, they are the people who will work against your efforts to improve yourself and reach your dreams. Your goal here is obvious: reduce contact or eliminate them from your life completely, if possible. Of course, critics and people who disagree are *not* necessarily toxic people, if their disagreement inspires us or encourages us to be better.

Next, identify those people that don't add much to your life. Perhaps they're there because they've always been there, but they neither hinder nor advance your overall goals. These people are great to have around, but you should try to prioritize spending time with those who more actively support and teach you, or who you enjoy mentoring.

Finally, the third group includes those who are on your side, and are there providing guidance, help, support or can teach you something. Even better if it's a mutual benefit! These are the kinds of people to prioritize in life. Attend networking events, seek out people in groups or clubs who are doing the same thing as you, or even consider asking someone more advanced or accomplished to give you advice or help.

Sensory-Rich Vision

Good plans matter, but before good plans comes a good vision. Ask any creator about their magnum opus and many of them will say that they saw the vision fully completed in their mind's eye *first*, long before they took the first step to bring it to life. Every innovator first sees a vision of what could be, and then works toward that.

But don't get too attached to the word "vision"—you have so many more sense that just sight! Enlist all your senses to conjure up an image of what you want to achieve, Make it real in your mind. Dwell on every detail. The thing is, people who self-sabotage, procrastinate, and operate below their potential do this anyway—except they do it negatively.

They vividly imagine scenarios of total failure. They dwell on possibilities—but only on the negative ones. This only fosters fear, doubt, anger, and apathy. Rather than being in a curious, proactive, creative, and receptive frame of mind, you're homing in on problems, almost setting yourself up for a bad outcome.

Set up a "vision board" where you paste collaged images that make you think of your goal. Position your board where you can see it constantly. Alternatively, spend time actively visualizing end goals, in detail. With closed eyes, focus all your attention on what it will look and feel like once you have accomplished your goal. Conjure up this sensory image with as much detail as possible. You may find that the vision is not as clear as you once assumed! Flesh out the details and you automatically sharpen up your goal—and adjust your plan for getting there.

Self-belief

If your self-esteem is in the dumps, you won't sustain motivation for very long. There are three main things you can do to take better care of your self-esteem. The first is to acknowledge and face rejection and failure, i.e. become to it. The second is to know how to self-monitor and give yourself a pep talk when necessary. The third is to practice self-care and gratitude— two things that have more in common than it may seem on the surface.

The prospect of failure, rejection or criticism can be behind our fear of trying. We weigh ourselves against the challenge ahead and find ourselves lacking. But we may undervalue ourselves and overvalue the challenge, or else wrongly assume that failure is the end of the world and something we can't possibly endure.

But is it? Rather than bolstering yourself by saying how everything is going to be okay, do the opposite: say that you might actually fail . . . but so what? You can handle it, you can try again, and failure doesn't define you. In fact, you *love* failure because it's the kindest teacher.

Mediation and mindfulness practice can help you keep a tab on your most precious resource of all—your mindset. If you notice yourself feeling doubtful or self-critical, remind yourself that you have absolute worth and value whether you succeed or not. What matters is your attitude and your actions. Keep curious, chin up, and keep going.

Finally, make sure your self-care is in order. Take enough rest. Be kind to yourself and learn to appreciate everything you have and are even as you're on the road to something bigger and better. Gratitude and compassion can make all the difference.

Planning and Organization

This is one of the easier aspects to cultivate in yourself.

- Tidy your desk and workspace— clutter drains your willpower and your focus
- Install apps on your PC or phone that prevent you from browsing the internet during fix periods, forcing you to focus on the task at hand
- Print out a large calendar to keep track of your month at a glance

- Commit to focusing on a maximum of three tasks per day, no more. Schedule these for the time you feel most energetic and deprioritize everything else
- As far as possible, automate smaller admin tasks so you don't have a million little things to remember and can focus on the bigger picture
- Be ruthless with paper—when you encounter a piece, act on it instantly (for example file it away) or get rid of it
- At the end of every week, sped a few moments writing down what you achieved, what you didn't, what you did well, and what you could do better. Ask what did *not* help forward your mission, and make a plan to remove or eliminate it in the coming week
- As much as you can, delegate. A big part of staying organized is making sure you're not putting too much on your plate
- Remember the 80/20 rule—around twenty percent of your actions are producing eighty percent of your results. Keep an eye on that twenty

percent, and downplay everything else

- If you do nothing else on this list, **STOP MULTITASKING**. Instead, do "deep work" and focus—it's better to do one thing extremely well than to fritter away time on a hundred smaller projects

Education and Skills

It's a little ironic—human beings want to be better, to improve and expand their horizons . . . but they are also fearful of change, hate not knowing things, and don't want to ever risk failure. Seems silly, huh?

Valuing education is about embracing the fact that if you're alive, you're always a newbie in some way or another. Learning involves a degree of discomfort, awkwardness, and effort. You can only access the benefits of further training and education if you're willing to do accept these.

To foster a real love and respect for learning, you need to make an effort. Push yourself. At the end of every week or month, ask yourself what you've learned. What are you curious about? Make a note and identify the ways you can learn more. Who knows more than you about this topic and what questions can you ask them? What does your failure tell you about how best to try again next time?

The next time you encounter something that looks challenging or too difficult, instead of shrugging and turning away from it, assume that you can understand it, with just a little effort. Enroll in free online courses to brush up on skills. See a new word in an article? Look it up in the dictionary. If someone says something interesting, don't pretend to know about it already to save face—ask them to tell you more. Opportunities to learn are literally everywhere—go online, get interested in a hobby, or dig deeper into those parts of your life that seem mysterious or difficult.

Oh, and there's on sure fire way to keep learning: **read**. Disciplined high achievers almost always share the same habit of reading, every day if possible.

Patient Perseverance

Doing all the above means nothing if you only keep it up for an afternoon and then wonder why your life is not magically transformed. Abandon the need for quick fixes and overnight success. There are no hacks or cheat codes (in fact, things that seem that way often cost more in the long run).

Instead, ask yourself regularly, "What's the smallest, *sustainable* change I can make?" Not the biggest quantum leap, not the grandest plan. But the action you can comfortably repeat day after day, month after month.

Think in terms of habits and behavioral change rather than flashy one-off achievements. Focus on process and not outcome.

For example, every day you could commit to walking for thirty minutes. You're not committing to running a marathon or losing fifty pounds. All you have to focus on each day is walking thirty minutes, that's it. You may certainly build up to the marathon or gradually lose all that weight, but that's not what you focus on each day, each moment. Just take a baby step each day, then repeat it the next day. Biting off more than you can chew only means you give up sooner!

If your motivation is really flagging, it's fine to take a break. But make it productive. Ask yourself if your goals and approach are really working, see if you can make any adjustments, and give yourself a fixed time to get back on the horse.

Seeing Work as Play

Watch your language! Don't say, "I have to do XYZ," but instead say, "I choose to do XYZ." In fact, don't call it work at all, if you can. You're learning, creating, growing. If possible, use certain gamification strategies to bring more fun and spontaneity into your "work."

Work outside for the afternoon or try a completely different approach. Experiment, play, and see what happens. Remember, nobody is *forcing* you to be self-disciplined. Rather, it's something you are deliberately pursuing because part of you already knows that, ultimately, life feels far more meaningful that way.

Rock-Solid Principles for Lasting Motivation and Self-Discipline

There is no ideal time to start.

"Great," you think, "this all sounds like a good idea. I'll give it a go sometime."

So many hopes and dreams die in that strange no-man's land called "someday." How many of us waste time and energy because we believe in holding out for some better moment to start somewhere far off in the future?

The status quo is comfortable, familiar, and already full in swing. It takes effort and discomfort to break that momentum. When you start telling yourself all the reasons why you can't begin yet? That's just plain old resistance. The right moment never actually comes, and in waiting for it, you delay starting indefinitely.

You might think that it makes more sense to wait until things would be easier. You can't begin writing your novel just yet because work is chaotic and will die down next month. Or you'll start applying for jobs soon but wait till the weekend when you have the time. Or worse, you'll just wait for things to improve in a general sort of way . . .

But the outcome is obvious—later down the line, there is some other reason preventing you from taking action, and so on forever.

The only wait forward is to act. Act even if you're unsure, even if you don't feel prepared (hint: you never will), and even if you're a bit scared. The whole point of taking a big step out your comfort zone is that it's unfamiliar and a little scary. Wait for it to not be scary and you'll be waiting a long, long time.

But go easy on yourself; you don't have to do it all at once, and you don't have to do it perfectly. You don't even have to like it as you do it! You just have to do it. In that sense, there's a lot less pressure on you than you maybe thought. Just take one small action in the right direction, and do not allow yourself to wriggle out of it.

Waiting for the ideal moment is a trick of the perfectionist mind. It speaks to an intolerance for being in process, for doing things inelegantly, or making mistakes. Think of it this way, though—the first stages of any endeavor often are embarrassing, difficult, slow, awkward or a little unpleasant. Why put all that off, when you could start now and get it over and done with? That brings us to:

Baby Steps, Not Quantum Leaps

Yes, you want to have a full vision of the end point. You need to know the goal you're striving for and hold it in your mind. But in the day to day, you can actually forget about all the grand plans and big ideas. That's because even the grandest plan is small, when seen on the day-to-day level. Think of Michelangelo painting the Sistine chapel— some days he would have spent just working on a tiny, unimpressive square inch, only to erase it again later.

You need to zoom out and have big vision, but you also need to zoom in and focus on all the tiny, countless steps that carry you bit by bit toward that big vision. If you only see the big vision all the time, you might feel completely overwhelmed with the daily tasks. How demotivating to see how much there is to still do! But if you dwell on this too long, you don't even begin.

When you pace yourself with small, achievable tasks that are done regularly and consistently, you build habits, which then work on their own, without the constant injection of willpower. What's more, you don't get discouraged, because every day you are not tasked with making a huge transformation—you just have to clear what's on your plate and start again fresh tomorrow.

Taking baby steps keeps you psychologically motivated and with good forward momentum, so you don't stall and give your old habits a chance to settle in again. Even if you only advance the tiniest bit, you still advance. Multiply that over a month or a year, and it quickly adds up.

So, if you're feeling overwhelmed or discouraged, just stop, take a breath, and break things down into smaller chunks. Do one chunk. Just one. If it still seems insurmountable, break it down further. If you're massively procrastinating on doing a project, tell yourself you don't have to do anything more than a minute of it, right now. Don't think about it, just start. Tell yourself you can stop after one minute. The thing is, when you get to the end of the minute, you have another choice: can you do one more minute? Maybe you can't. But chances are, you can. Somehow, it's easier to do sixty small increments this way rather than forcing yourself to sit down for a full hour. In practice, momentum takes over after a while and you find the resistance drops away. But you have to take that first step.

Flex Your Intrinsic Motivation, Not Your Extrinsic

Here's the difference. Extrinsic motivation comes from outside, i.e. from rewards or punishments that come from others or the environment, while intrinsic motivation comes from within you, i.e. from your own motivation, passion, or commitment. So, if a child does their homework because they enjoy the material and like the satisfaction of mastering the task, that's intrinsic motivation. It's also intrinsic motivation if they feel fundamentally unworthy and are trying to prove to themselves that they can do it.

But if the child does it because they'll get in trouble with the teacher if they don't, or because they like the praise they receive from their parents when they do, this is extrinsic motivation. In life, people are motivated to do things for a mix of complex reasons, some of them not understandable, even to them. But on the whole, when it comes to self-discipline and motivated life, you need to aim for intrinsic motivation.

But let's be honest, being driven by greed, fear, peer pressure, and so on *will* get you somewhere, at least initially. Employees do work under the threat of being fired if they don't, and much good has been accomplished in the world even if for all the wrong reasons!

How can we apply this knowledge?

There is nothing wrong with extrinsic motivators, but they are seldom enough on their own, and the effect they produce is rarely sustained. Extrinsic motivation is great to use for tasks you simply cannot muster sincere motivation for, like brushing your teeth daily or clearing your gutters in winter. You don't need to be passionate about either of these tasks, you just need to do them, and if fear of what happens if you don't is all that motivates you, so be it.

But for more important areas of life, intrinsic motivation is more appropriate. You need to be connected to your values, to your big WHY, and if you aren't, chances are you're working with external motivation. Periodically ask yourself, "What's driving me right now?" Intrinsic or extrinsic motivators can be either positive or negative, or a blend. But you need to understand what is powering your action and take control. This requires honesty and self-awareness. Ask yourself:

- Would I continue to do this if I wasn't paid or nobody noticed/cared?
- Do I find value in this activity itself, or am I just doing it to get to the end result?

- Am I acting out of fear, insecurity, self-doubt, or a desire for approval?
- What are my goals and values, and are these mine or did I borrow them from someone else?

Lead Yourself Not into Temptation

The world is made of it. Every supermarket is bursting with addictive, unhealthy food. You carry around a mobile phone expressly designed to capture and hold your attention no matter what. There is constant distraction and the invitation to indulge in seemingly endless desires. Friends and family might lure you away from your best laid plans, or you may succumb to an extra episode of whatever addictive show is on Netflix, or you simply bounce from one compulsive habit to the next, your willpower slackening all the while.

It's a fact of life. Temptation is not going away. So, we need to learn to deal with it. Willpower is a limited quantity and needs to be budgeted wisely. You *can* bravely resist in the face of temptation, but only for so long. A far better strategy is to position yourself so that you're exposed to as little temptation as possible from the outset. In other words, avoid it.

Make it easier to stick to your commitments than to give in to temptation. The classic example is to simply not keep unhealthy snacks at home to stop yourself guzzling them. In effect, you're allowing yourself to have unhealthy snacks—but only if you get in your car and go out and buy them there and then. So, it's too hard to act without discipline, and acting with discipline is the default. Set up as much of your life in this was as possible.

- Cut your credit card in half, give it to someone else to keep, or freeze it (yes, in a block of ice in the freezer!) so you can't access it easily ad overspend.
- Put your alarm on the other side of the room so you need to physically get up to turn it off and avoid the temptation to lay in bed hitting snooze a dozen times.
- If you're tempted to be unfaithful, avoid that person entirely. (Not the nicest topic, but you get the idea— why give yourself the chance to creep

closer and closer to what you know is a bad idea?)

An important final tip: if you *do* give in to temptation? No big deal. Forgive yourself, quickly, and get right back on the wagon. Whatever you do, don't beat yourself up with guilt and shame . . . and then say something like, "Well, I've already ruined everything, might as well give up!" Don't let a small temptation turn into a bigger one.

Cull Distractions

You already know not to multitask, and to put your focus into ideally just one project at a time. Light beams, when focused onto a single point, act like a laser, which can cut through metal. When unfocused, those same light beams are weak and diffuse, barely even illuminating what they fall on.

In a way, being focused and being self-disciplined are one and the same thing. Discipline is the constant effort required to pull all the light beams into one place, in essence saying *no* to countless distractions so you can say *yes* to the single goal you've identified as more valuable.

Here's a hard-to-swallow truth: many of us don't even realize a) that our attention is being derailed and b) what exactly is derailing it.

The first step is to simply recognize that your mind is being pulled away from its task, and the next is to identify what is the cause. Only when you've done both of these things can you do anything to reclaim your attention again. Sadly, the modern world is designed to distract, numb, and pacify you—exactly the opposite state of mind required to reach your goals.

Common distractions include phones and devices (turn them to silent, put them in another room, or disable notifications), TV (turn it off *immediately* once your show is finished, or avoid it completely), or an environment that is uncomfortable and cluttered (use noise canceling earphones, put up a Do Not Disturb sign, or clear your desk so it only contains materials for the task at hand). Slow down and become hyperconscious of where your attention is going. Get into the habit of asking yourself,

"Is this what I want to be focusing on right now?"

Monitor Impulses with Mindfulness

To extend the idea about distraction, use the power of mindfulness to watch your fleeting attention, and see where it goes and why. Meditation and mindfulness practice are great for whatever ails you, but they're especially useful if you feel that your mind is buys, fractured, uncontrolled, or overrun with impulses it can't resist.

Try this. Set a timer for yourself, let's say ten minutes, where you logically know that the *only thing you need to worry about* is the project in front of you, whatever it is. Now, watch your attention. Notice if any impulses arise to switch focus to something else (check your phone, open a new browser to look at YouTube, go look for a snack . . .). Tell yourself that during these ten minutes, you don't *have to* work on your project, but you absolutely cannot do anything else.

If your mind wanders, notice it, and bring it back to task again. It's just for ten minutes (actually, this will seem like eternity if you're used to getting distracted!). Try to notice that impulses are just that—brief moments of desire that die away again pretty quickly. Also notice that you're not compelled to follow each and every one of them. The more you can practice looking at an urge objectively and calmly deciding not to pursue, the less of a hold distractions will have on you. You can simply shrug and say, "Oh, hello, distraction. Are you well? Great. Now go away."

Practicing formal meditation will help strengthen this muscle even further. Keep bringing awareness to temptations and distractions and then consistently decide where *you* want to put your awareness. There's no need for judgment or interpretation, however ("You're such a distractable idiot. *Focus* for heaven's sake!"); simply notice and adjust. Your focused attention is like any muscle—it strengthens with consistent use.

Make Friends with Discomfort

Let's say you make a plan to lose weight and fill your head with the lovely end result: you feeling slim and trim and pleased with yourself. You start a diet and exercise plan, and you feel great, but at the first hurdle, you stumble and go back to your old ways. Why? It's because of the clash between that great feeling ("Hooray, I lost weight!") and the cold hard reality of obstacles, challenge, and discomfort getting in your way ("Hm, this gym membership is more expensive than I thought . . .").

In other words, you didn't expect discomfort, so you were thrown off course when it appeared. But the thing is, it always does appear! By definition, leaving our comfort zone is uncomfortable. Yes, you're going to feel great when you achieve your goal . . . but in the meantime, you're probably going to feel worse than if you'd done nothing at all.

Read that last sentence again: *improving yourself or seeking out a goal is going to be more uncomfortable than the status quo.* This is not a flaw, but a feature. If you don't anticipate and plan for it, it will undermine you every time. What can you do to get around this?

Do the opposite: don't just anticipate discomfort, but *relish* it. Seek it out. When you go on a diet, don't fill your head with images of how great it'll be to be thinner; instead, dwell on the fact that you will sometimes feel hungry, lazy, or tempted to give up. You release the hold these feelings have on you when you can accept them and prepare for them.

See discomfort as evidence of change. If you feel stupid, good—it's a sign you're in the perfect environment to learn. Those pangs and aches and worries and doubts? Welcome them—they are the price you are paying for striving for better. See what happens if you take a cold shower on purpose. See what it feels like to delay gratification for a while. Laugh at yourself if you feel scared or lazy. After all, it's only discomfort—it won't kill you!

Use the Power of Visualization

Let's return to the goal of losing weight. On the one hand, you have the enticing vision of you at your goal weight, on the other hand you have a temptation right in front of you—let's say an enormous slice of cake your friend has just offered you. Often, we choose the immediately satisfying option instead (cake, now) over the one that will materialize later (reaching our goal) simply because we are unable to really appreciate the value of the goal that is delayed in the future. In other words, we often choose one hundred dollars now instead of two hundred dollars later—it's not logical, but our brain has a bias for immediate gratification, overvaluing what's right in front of us.

The human tendency is to *under*value those benefits that only materialize in the future. We focus only on the present—and actually, judging by what's in the moment alone, a piece of cake IS better than no piece of cake! But you can see that in doing this, you are basically giving yourself up to the noisiest and most alluring distraction or temptation in your immediate environment. It's a recipe for lack of focus and lack of purpose. What you get is a string of temporarily pleasing moments but zero sense of anything amounting to much in the long term.

There's one good way to counteract this: use your imagination. By visualizing your end goal with clarity, you bring the benefits more concretely into the present moment. So, the comparison is really: do you want this nice cake, or do you want to feel fit, healthy, and attractive after you've lost weight? This is a much more realistic way of looking at things.

A good habit is to teach yourself to pause before any decision and recall your goals and intentions. Go quiet within and conjure up the image of what you're trying to accomplish and why. Build this up internally. Feel how much you want it. See how good it's going to be once you get there. Now open your eyes and look at the temptation—is it *really* worth you derailing all your plans for?

Let Your Future Self Lead You

A variation on this is to pay attention to the version of you that will arise if you achieve your goal. Imagine the person who you'd like to become, the one in a potential future who has achieved what you want to achieve. Spend some time fleshing this person out. What are they doing, thinking, feeling? Where do they live, who are they with? In as much detail as possible, visualize this imaginary future you.

Now, let this version of yourself give your *present* version of yourself a pep talk. You see, in the moment, it's the urges, addictions and transient desires that speak the strongest, but what would your future self say about the slice of cake? What advice would they give you? From *that* point of view, look at your options, and make a decision.

By doing this, you're again bringing the intangible and abstract future into the present where you can weigh it up properly. You might gobble the cake in the moment, and love it, but it's your future self who feels bad about it and guilty for yet again sabotaging their bigger, more important goals. So listen to that voice instead.

It's easy to look at temptations for their immediate virtues and forget about their future costs. Invert this and deliberately downplay the instant gratification and amplify the long-term consequences. So, when you look at a piece of cake, you don't see something delicious and amazing; you see the guilt, bad feeling, and lack of belief in yourself for not having discipline. You see yourself starting all over again, no closer to your goal than you were before. Suddenly, the cake doesn't look all that great.

Know How to Bounce Back after You Mess Up

Yes, you will face distractions. Yes, you will encounter discomfort. The path will be slow and sometimes boring, with little reward in the present moment. And here's another thing: you *will* make a mistake.

On your journey, expect that you will succumb at some point or other to temptation, or you will take three steps back after taking two forward. Now, this doesn't mean you're doing anything wrong. It isn't a sign that the goal you've set is too hard, or evidence that you'd better just give everything up and not even bother. It's not permission to slack or make excuses for yourself, and it's not an invitation to turn a small slip up into a big one (i.e. "I've had one slice of cake already. What's another?").

It's just a normal, expected part of the process. You're not wrong or bad; you're just trying to do something intrinsically difficult—change. Things won't always go to plan. Sometimes you'll fall a little short or be disappointed in the outcome. Sometimes you'll be tired or frustrated or disorganized and not do as well as you imagined.

So what?

Forgiveness in these moments is not an excuse—the opposite in fact. It's the state of mind that allows you to get back into things as quickly as possible. If you're wallowing in self-pity or self-hatred, you're only delaying getting back to work. You can feel upset, certainly, but don't let that stop you from getting proactive: acknowledge that you failed, look for the reason why, and commit to doing better next time. There really is no other way forward.

Life will knock you down sometimes, but the longer you stay down, the easier it is for old mental habits to take hold again. Don't skip a beat or lose any momentum, just get back up again and carry on. Forgiveness is a gift you give to yourself—it says, "Yes, that was bad, but I'm going to let the negativity go and focus on the good." And then you do it.

Don't aim for perfection—perfection is fragile, impossible, anxiety-provoking. Instead, tune your attention to what can be done right now to get you facing the right direction and walking back on your right path again. You may be surprised just how comforting it is to take back control in this way.

Takeaways

- Working with the limitations of your own brain requires an honest appraisal of where you are and how you're functioning. Make it a habit to routinely assess yourself on the following aspects, on a scale of one to ten: Sense of purpose, the presence of positive mentors, sensory rich vision, self-belief, planning and organization, education and skills, patient perseverance, and the ability to see work as play.

- This kind of self-reflection allows you to see exactly what areas you need to work on and see whether your efforts are resulting in progress.
- Depending on which aspects you identify as under-developed, you can do a lot to improve.
- For a stronger sense of purpose, you'll need to work on self-knowledge, and dig deep into your genuine values. To find positive mentors, reach out to others and network, or simply ask for help and advice from accomplished people.
- To develop sensory rich vision, make a goal collage or practice visualization to conjure up a vivid, five-sense image of the end you're aiming for. To increase self-belief, actively court failure and rejection—to prove to yourself that your worth as a person doesn't stem from these things. Meditation, mindfulness, and self-care also go a long way to cultivating self-compassion.
- To have better planning and organization, start by decluttering both your mind and workspace to cut down on distractions. Set up habits that allow you to atomate, delegate and concentrate.

- To build skills and education, keep reading. Become curious, and ask questions, learning where you can. To improve patience and perseverance, focus on the smallest, *sustainable* change you can make and keep up every day. To see work as play, change your language. Don't say, "I have to do XYZ," but instead say, "I choose to do XYZ." Remember, nobody is forcing you to be the best version of yourself.

- Focus on a few main principles for lasting motivation. These include not waiting for a right time, taking baby steps, working from intrinsic motivation, avoid temptation outright, cutting distractions, monitoring impulses with mindfulness, visualizing in detail our goal, getting comfortable with being uncomfortable, and allowing our future selves to advise and guide our present selves.

- Finally, the most important may be to recognize that you will slip up, but will always be ready to forgive, learn from mistakes, and move on to be better next time.

Chapter 5. Daily Habits

Every once in a while, a writer will come across something called "writer's block." This is a mental state in which the words just can't be squeezed out onto the paper, and no matter how hard they try, they can't think of what they want to write. It's like trying to extract water from a stone. People with this condition can go *months* without writing, to the extent that writing becomes something they don't even *do*.

But in most of these cases, writer's block can be overcome quite simply by aiming to write 750 words of nonsense every day.

Note that this is a drastically different aim than a writer would traditionally have.

Normally, words don't flow because they are too precious; some writers feel that every word, comma, and phrase makes a huge impact. Thus, the pressure to be great builds the longer they are withheld, and at this point, it starts to sound like we're back in that cycle of laziness, doesn't it? A writer may hold the belief that each word written needs to be literary gold, and then the avoidance begins. You couldn't possibly write junk, so you don't write at all.

But if you set the expectation that most of what you write *will be* junk, suddenly you'll be free to start typing because it simply doesn't matter. Junk will always junk, so there's no need to be precious or careful about it. All it takes is an excuse to start typing, and suddenly you far exceed the 750-word goal you set.

When we talk about habits, we are talking about default behaviors that help you reach your intentions. Here, the 750-word goal conditions your brain into a writing mentality so that you're not just sitting around waiting for inspiration to come.

You're making it a daily practice so that writing becomes easier. Importantly, your habit isn't "write the great American novel every day" but simply "write 750 words. *Any* words."

If you are constantly in the habit of writing, no matter what, then when you do get a great idea, you put it down. You're already in a great momentum, and the flow isn't interrupted. There is no effort in writing 750 words of nonsense—but in doing so you build an automatic habit in yourself that lays a fertile ground for writing that is not nonsense at all.

The best reinforcers you can provide yourself to maintain self-discipline and self-control are good habits. Unfortunately, we can start to go wayward when we aren't tied to any sort of guiding principle. A habit helps because it anchors you and removes off-the-cuff decision-making from the equation. In other words, you do the thing, no matter what. You know how you get up in the morning and brush your teeth no matter what? You can do almost any behavior with that same level of automaticity. The less responsibility you put on your sense of doing the right thing, the better off you will be. This chapter looks at some of the principles and strategies in developing helpful self-discipline habits.

Make a Formula

Something that damages self-discipline is when you look at it purely as, "I need to get off my butt." Obviously, that goes without saying, but it's not something that is helpful if you don't actually get off your butt immediately. If you stay planted, what then? You had better have some more weapons in your arsenal against laziness.

Similar to the cycle of laziness we discussed in an earlier chapter, we should seek to better understand what goes into our lack of self-discipline. Instead of a cycle, this time we turn to a formula to comprehend the different forces at play. A formula can sometimes be more helpful because it can tell you exactly what elements are involved and what you need to change. A recipe can tell you just how many eggs and how much flour to put in a cake; a formula here can do the same thing for your self-discipline. Sometimes you might realize that you are setting yourself up for failure by neglecting the eggs entirely, or trying to bake the cake in a rice cooker. You may not need to change much, just re-direct your efforts to what is important.

Formula-making happens in much the same way a scientist or mathematician goes about their work with a series of set procedures and methods to test their theories and solve problems. And just like scientists, you can manipulate and play with the quantities of each variable to achieve the effect that you want.

The only difference between scientific formulae and the one I'm talking about is that you're not using hard data, numbers, or mathematic standards to build the elements of your formula—instead, you're substituting your values, qualities, and external factors for numbers and functions. The concept is to replace the individual variables of something like $E = mc^2$ with more abstract, technically incalculable parts of your experience—things like motivation and beliefs and relationships between the two. You then incorporate this formula and base your decisions and actions around it, making adjustments or tweaks to the formula as you go until it's as right for you as possible.

The following is a helpful and fairly straightforward formula to explain my approach and beliefs about self-discipline:

SD = (PeM + PoB) - (dc + ds)

Spelled out a bit more:

Self-discipline = (personal motivation + positive benefits) – (discomfort + distractions)

This formula represents my concept of **self-discipline (SD)** and the individual elements that comprise it. The measure of self-discipline is the difference between positive forces and negative forces. As long as the sum on the right side turns out positive, then you will have self-discipline. If not, then it's time to pay attention to each of the variables to find out why it's *not* positive. The positives are represented as *(PeM + PoB)*, and the negatives are *(dc + ds)*.

Personal motivation *(PeM)*: This is why you care about something, why it's important to you, and what purpose will it serve? How satisfied and fulfilled will it make you? What does eating healthier represent to you? This is an internal quantity.

Positive benefits/impact of action *(PoB)*: What good will come from a certain action or operation? What gains will it result in, as tangibly as you can describe? Ideally there is both a short- and long-term component to this. What physical changes can you expect from eating healthier? This is a more external quantity, though it can also be internal.

Mental or physical discomfort *(dc)*: What kinds of physical or mental fatigue, pain, fear, trouble, or excuse-making are causing you to resist action? What will you lose by acting, and what negatives will you necessarily have to experience? How much physical discomfort of hunger and mental discomfort of restriction will you have to suffer? How well will you be able to deal with them? At the end of all of this, how will your mental and physical states of being fare—realistically and without forecasting doom?

Distractions *(ds)*: What unconscious or unintended diversions or hindrances might cause your attention to stray from the work you need to do? How many birthdays or parties will you have to endure in your quest to eat healthy? What concrete factors threaten to come between your intentions and actions?

Self-discipline ends up being the value of motives and positive results, minus the trouble and distractions that could thwart one from action. Putting this formula into action, the goal is to manipulate the positive forces so they'll outweigh the negatives, making for positive or better self-discipline. Along the way, you might realize that you've been neglecting one or two factors, heavily skewing the formula out of your favor.

SD = (PeM+PoB) − (dc + ds). Let's put that formula in action to provide inspiration for a habit of self-discipline that one might want to develop: quitting smoking.

Personal motivation (PeM). These are internal reasons that make one think quitting smoking is a good idea—why are they making that decision? They may have noticed they're short of breath or coughing a lot. Maybe one of their parents died from lung cancer as a result of lifelong smoking. They may want to be more physically active and want to make it as easy on themselves as they can. Or perhaps they're feeling like pariahs for being a smoker—peer pressure in this case would be a *positive* motivator. *Numeric value: 8/10*

Positive benefits (PoB). The attainment of all those goals in "personal motivation" would be a big benefit. It can take as little as a year for a long-time smoker's lungs to get back to normal. They'd also save a lot of money, not have a bunch of clothes that smell like smoke, be less self-conscious around non-smoking friends, feel less guilty, and feel a sense of pride after beating the addiction. *Numeric value: 5/10*

You would think that there are fairly compelling arguments for quitting. But what about the negative portion of the formula?

Mental/physical discomfort (dc). Someone quitting smoking might feel the pangs of physical withdrawal and be subject to cravings for a while. This is probably an understatement—they'll feel intense longing and perhaps even pain. They will probably fixate on smoking more than is healthy and feel incomplete without a cigarette. They may also feel that they have lost their method of stress relief. Don't underestimate these. *Numeric value: 9/10*

Potential distractions (ds). These would be anything that temporarily takes one's mind off the task of quitting smoking, making them forget about it enough to justify or allow themselves to falter. This could be a social situation where there's a lot of smokers or a stressful situation that might spur them to soothe themselves with a cigarette—anything that draws them away from being able to refuse to smoke. *Numeric value: 4/10*

The goal in this particular equation, then, is to maximize the positives and minimize the negatives. Try as much as possible to place a numeric value on each factor and manipulate the balance so that the positives overpower the negatives. The harder the data one uses, the easier it will be to "rank" each factor, though it is not always possible to quantify feelings and emotions.

For example, in our quitting-smoking example, the smoker could figure out how much money they'd be saving—maybe they've worked out that they spend between $250 and $300 a month on tobacco. Or they could calculate the health benefits: the amount of time they might spend getting more physical exercise or by how much their blood pressure, breathing rate, or daily walking steps might improve. And they should be fearless and honest about the negatives: how much weight might they gain? How strongly will the triggers be felt on a scale of one to ten?

If they can assign a numeric value to all the aspects of their experience, they'll have a way to track their progress and manage their expectations. And again, the goal is to make the positive results more "valuable" or higher than the negatives. If they aren't, then they need to manipulate the equation to make sure they are by finding *more* motivators or benefits or by decreasing the negative values in some way.

The *SD = (PeM+PoB) – (dc + ds)* formula can cover most instances in which you want to institute change. But a formula that is more tailored to your specific circumstances will work even better. You might have different elements that are more relevant to you than motivation, benefits, discomfort, or distractions—or you might want to be more specific about certain factors. Here's an example.

Time. Scheduling is a huge priority for many of us. You may want to factor in the expected amount of time you'll need to devote to working on your situation. How much can you truly allot to your goal?

Expense. For some efforts you might have to spend a little cash. In the smoking example, you might have to fork over some money for nicotine gum for a little while. But you'd also save some money from not buying cigarettes. You can also include opportunity costs here as an expense on time.

Emotional improvement. Although feelings are hard to quantify a lot of the time, if you're keenly in touch with your emotional status you might be able to ascribe values to your good and bad feelings. Is the anxiety that quitting smoking produces more value than the increased energy or relief you might feel? Perhaps you only want to focus on one specific benefit and nothing else matters at the moment.

The possibilities for what criteria you use for your own formula are endless. You have a lot of room to be creative about the factors that influence you the most. Figure out how strongly each of them relates to your own personality and beliefs and assign them a numeric value to see what you need to eliminate, increase, or otherwise manipulate.

With all your options, you may come up with a complicated formula with dozens of variables. That might be good for analysis, but not in practice. The fewer moving parts there are to your formula, the more manageable it is—after all, both the cycle of laziness and this formula show that it's not so complex.

The If-Then Technique

A helpful habit that directly deals with the fork in the road that may or may not lead to self-discipline is the *if-then technique*. This is also sometimes known as an *implementation intention*—in other words, making your intention easy to implement. The *if* portion corresponds to an everyday event occurring, while the *then* portion corresponds to the self-disciplined action you desire.

The simple fact is that there's a big gap between knowing what you want to do and actually getting it done. Whatever the case—distractions, inefficiencies, or procrastination—making the decision beforehand will make it easier.

If-then statements take the following form: if X happens, then I will do Y. That's it. This is something you decide in advance, and there are two primary ways to use it. This makes it easier to build self-discipline because all you have to do is plug your desired action in as a natural consequence of something that is certain to happen. When actions are chained and given forethought, they tend to happen. When actions are left to individual negotiations on willpower in the fleeting moment, they tend to not happen.

As a quick example, *if* it is 3:00 p.m. on Sunday, *then* you will call your mother (for some of us, this might require massive self-discipline). Or *if* it is 3:00 p.m., *then* you will drink two liters of water, or if it is 9:00 p.m., then you will floss your teeth. These are examples of when you use if-then to accomplish a specific goal, the first type of use. X can be whatever event, time, or occurrence you choose that happens on a daily basis, and Y is the specific action that you will take.

The if-then statement simply takes your goals out of the ether and ties them to concrete moments in your day. Rather than wrangle the question anew each time it's 3:00 p.m., you just consult your life "rule" and call your mother. Cause and effect. A habit to eat healthier and drink more water has a set prescription, for instance, or a vow to have better dental health is carried out every day because it is contingent upon a daily occurrence.

Instead of generalities, you get a set time and place for when to act. In a way, it takes a lot out of your hands and makes the decision for you. Is it 3:00 p.m.? Then it's tie to drink water, period. Imagine that you are looking at an empty planner and trying to decide when to make a doctor's appointment. Now imagine that you are trying to decide when to make the appointment, but you only have one slot open in your entire week. Sometimes, alleged freedom makes your task more difficult.

It seems simplistic, and it is, but it has been shown that you are two to three times more likely to succeed if you use an if-then plan than if you don't. In one study, ninety-one percent of people who used an if-then plan stuck to an exercise program versus thirty-nine of non-planners. Peter Gollwitzer, the NYU psychologist who first articulated the power of if-then planning, recently reviewed results from ninety-four studies that used the technique and found significantly higher success rates for just about every goal you can think of, from using public transportation more frequently to avoiding stereotypical and prejudicial thoughts.

The primary reason if-then statements work so well is because they speak the language of your brain, which is the language of contingencies. Humans are good at encoding information in "If X, then Y" terms and using this process (often unconsciously) to guide our behavior. It's the basis of decision-making, which is often subconscious and instantaneous. Deciding exactly when and where you will act on your goal creates a link in your brain between the situation or cue (the *if*) and the behavior that should follow (the *then*).

Suppose your significant other has been giving you a hard time about forgetting to text to inform them that you will be working late and not make dinner. So you make an if-then plan: if it is 6:00 p.m. and I'm at work, then I will text my significant other. Now the situation "6:00 p.m. at work" is wired in your brain directly to the action "text my sugar bear."

Then the situation or cue "6:00 p.m. at work" becomes highly activated. Below your awareness, your brain starts scanning the environment, searching for the situation in the "if" part of your plan. Once the "if" part of your plan happens, the "then" part follows *automatically*. You don't *have* to consciously monitor your goal, which means your plans get carried out even when you are preoccupied.

The best part is that by detecting situations and directing behavior without conscious effort, if-then plans are far less taxing and require less willpower than mere resolutions. They enable us to conserve our self-discipline for when it's really needed and compensate for it when we don't have enough.

The second use of the if-then statement is also related to achieving a specific goal, in particular, how to avoid *failing* at that goal. You would still use "if X, then Y," but X would be an unexpected situation that you want to maintain control in and deal with. In the first use, X is simply any everyday situation, occurrence, or event. Here, X is something that may not happen but you want to be prepared for.

For instance, if you want to create a habit of drinking water, *if* you eat out at a restaurant, *then* you will get water with lemon only. That's a situation that isn't certain to occur, but it helps you adhere to your habit from the opposite end.

Complete these statements *before* you are in a dire situation, and you can see how they work for you. It is like creating a rule for yourself to abide by. If you've given it thought beforehand, you can default to that guideline and not have to try to make a risky decision in the heat of the moment. Anticipate what's going to happen, and you are a step ahead of the game.

As another example, suppose it's your birthday, but you're on a strict diet and your office has a thing for surprise parties so you'll probably be getting a cake. "If they brought cake, then I'll turn it down and immediately drink a big glass of water." Alternatively, you could be having a problem with procrastination, and you're settling in for a big project you have to finish. You could say, "If the phone rings, then I'll ignore it until I'm done."

You can get more detailed with these statements and can prepare them for situations with more significance or danger than the above examples. But whatever the case, the if-then technique forces you to project yourself into common scenarios that could trigger reversion to a lack of willpower—and makes you plan for those triggers. It takes away your residuals of false justification and excuses for doing the wrong thing (or doing nothing) and sharpens your commitment to meeting your goals.

Know Your Discipline Style

Something that's important to know before you engage in all this planning and scheming to achieve your goals is your *style* of discipline. And of course, once you know, that's when you make it a habit.

There are two primary approaches people take to self-discipline: moderation and abstinence. Each has its merits and negatives, and no approach works for everyone.

Let's start with the definitions of these words. According to Oxford Dictionaries, *moderation* is "the avoidance of excess or extremes." You'll have only one scoop of ice cream. You know when you're too drunk to keep drinking. You can limit yourself to one hour of television a day.

Merriam-Webster defines *abstinence* as "the habit of not doing or having something that is wanted or desirable." No ice cream allowed. No games. No television. No alcohol. No fun.

Let's start with moderation. Moderation, if you can handle it, is a strategy to have your cake and eat it too. Eating dessert in moderation is a way to enjoy sweets without going overboard. You wouldn't want to eat multiple desserts every single day, as there may be health, weight, and blood sugar consequences. But a dessert every now and then is acceptable. This is moderation in action. You've heard the maxim "everything in moderation," which generally supports the freedom to indulge without *over*indulging.

So what is the application of moderation in the self-discipline realm? If you are trying to accomplish a task, you can take breaks along the way. You can indulge in your distractions, take a walk, and even procrastinate a little bit. In moderation, you get a mental break, you refresh yourself, and then you start again, reenergized. There's a timeline, and as long as you're basically adhering to it, then all is well. Of course, it might be said that you need a decent degree of innate self-discipline to engage in this strategy. If so, you can save yourself from the pain of abstinence that others might encourage—it would probably drive you insane and not work for you.

Moderation can give you freedom—the freedom of choice and flexibility to adapt to your circumstances and desires. It's the happy medium between the extremes. You don't have to go all or nothing when you're able to find that "sweet spot" in between. Of course, this comes with a rather large caveat. If you identify with this description of moderated self-discipline, it's because you feel that you can regulate yourself well enough that indulging won't completely throw you off. Just imagine a chronic alcoholic or addict of any kind—a moderated approach probably isn't ideal for them.

That's where abstinence comes in. For those with a weaker sense of self-discipline, an inability to regain focus in a timely manner, unfamiliarity with flexing their self-discipline muscle, or simply seeking a simpler approach, abstinence is the way to go. You might be able to stop the action itself, but it may occupy your brain afterward for a detrimental amount of time.

Thus, it's easier to set a blanket rule for yourself instead of having to rein yourself in instance by instance and negotiate with your desires and impulses. When you have to keep telling yourself no, a lapse in judgment is far more likely to occur than when you already know the answer is no. Sometimes *complete lacking* provides less suffering than having to stop before you are fully satisfied. An addict needs to stay away because they lack the ability to control themselves in that environment or context, so it's easier to position themselves for success by keeping their temptations at arm's length.

Another example is so-called *screen time*. At times, it seems as if today's society has us in front of a screen at all hours of the day. We have smartphones, tablets, television, laptops, and e-readers, and one of them is never more than an arm's length away.

While many people *can* moderate their screen time, not everyone has that ability. If you are a gamer, you may need to give up gaming completely in order to be able to function—otherwise, the gamer can often be heard saying, "Just another round," or,

"Just another five minutes!" Similarly, some people leave or give up social media for good because they know it's impossible to just hop on there for thirty seconds and push it completely out of their minds.

Abstinence, for some, is the simplest, surest, and easiest approach. You don't have the struggle of trying to *stop*, rather just *not starting*. Abstinence can also offer you freedom—freedom from tough choices and freedom from punishing yourself for trying to moderate or control your behavior and potentially failing.

What's the answer to improving self-discipline—moderation or abstinence? Should you try to pick one over the other? Which one is "better"? Is it always an either/or proposition? Is it just as easy as saying, "If you can handle it, moderation. If not, abstinence"?

There are no easy answers to these questions. To some degree, you need to know yourself. Do you have a tendency for extremes? Do you go all-or-nothing when approaching a task or goal? Or are you able to cut yourself off at a given milestone or time point? How easily can you redirect your energies toward a task? Instead of answering these questions off the cuff, answer them by thinking about examples of your past behavior—only actions matter here, not intentions.

Maybe we can think of this as a process. The first step would be abstinence. While we work on our willpower, you can completely avoid your triggers and distractions. As we mature and develop our discipline, then we can consider moderation. This is otherwise known as going "cold turkey." You might find that you can completely control yourself after this learning period, and no further reinforcement is needed.

On the other hand, the opposite process (moderation to abstinence) is also valid as a process of weaning yourself off of something. Here, the end goal would be complete abstinence. Whatever the case, understand that you probably lean naturally toward one over the other, so don't try to be someone that you're not.

Utilize Peer Pressure

As a teenager, you were probably warned of the pitfalls of peer pressure. And yet you still probably uttered the words, "But *everyone* else is doing it," more than once because it was nearly impossible to resist at the time. The fact of the matter is that we decide far less on our own than we think. We are victims of our social and physical environments.

Peer pressure is the direct influence upon someone by his or her social circle. In the teenage context, it's almost always talked about in the negative sense. Even as adults, we may still experience peer pressure in some of the more negative ways we did as teens. It's often in the sense of "keeping up with the Joneses."

But is there a positive side to peer pressure? Like most things, it all depends on whether you can control it or you become controlled by it. And that depends on your honest awareness of it. Peer pressure in self-discipline allows you to partially place your burden on others— which is amazing because it means self-discipline doesn't have to be something you carry internally and individually anymore.

We've previously discussed that the environment makes a difference in your discipline, and one aspect of environment includes the people around you. At the basic level, this means you have to be proactive and conscious about whom you surround yourself with. You don't have to start from zero, but at least recognize that there are certainly people who will push you up as well as drag you down. It is within your control to surround yourself with the most disciplined and motivated people, which will inevitably rub off on you. You may not be able to choose your family or coworkers, but the people you spend your free time with are up for grabs.

Aside from the general level of support you find in your social atmosphere, there are a variety of ways to take advantage of positive peer pressure. We can utilize mentors or role models. We can create accountability groups or partners.

An accountability partner is someone who helps keep you on track toward your goals. You check in or report to them, and you update them on your progress or lapses.

You are more likely to work toward your goals and stay on course if you have someone to whom you're accountable. It can be a mutual relationship (working toward similar goals), or they can simply act as your daily or weekly alarm clock.

When looking for an accountability partner, you want someone who won't buy your excuses or rationalizations. They should be instructed to take a black or white view on you—you either did something or not, and you either abstained from something or not. The more room you leave for flexibility, the more you might as well not use an accountability partner. This should be a person whom you trust and someone who isn't afraid to "tell it like it is." You want someone who won't judge you, but you also want someone who won't sugarcoat the tough stuff.

This is the person whom you call every day before you start your gym workout to check in. You're no longer letting yourself down; you're letting someone else down, so the stakes are higher as well.

You also want someone who is goal-oriented and is able to act as a good influence on you. Their successes can be things that help and motivate you to your own wins. Perhaps you even start to compete with them. Your accountability partner should both help you through your obstacles and celebrate your successes with you.

Frequent contact is preferable, because you leave less room for cycles of lapses and then trying to compensate for them. Frequent contact encourages better consistency. It's also a good idea to articulate a set duration of the relationship. Having a deadline creates a small sense of urgency—or at least the importance of progress; having no deadline can simply make matters too relaxed and slow-paced for any real progress to occur.

This important person seems elusive, but potential accountability partners are all around you. Remember, they just need to be willing to be honest with you. Think about friends and acquaintances that might fit the bill for what you need. Ask your partner, family, or circle of friends if they have suggestions for you. Some workplaces or professional programs have mentor programs where you can be paired with a colleague. You don't actually have to know them personally.

If this idea seems too bizarre or invasive, another approach is to find a role model, someone you respect and has had success in the area you're working on. This would be a person you would like to emulate; you don't have to interact with them. You can approach situations in your life and ask, "What would this person do in a situation of this nature?" Again, you don't have to actually know this person; the most important part is that they possess traits that you admire.

You can imagine this person when you start to stumble with your self-discipline. Detach yourself from the immediacy of the situation and put yourself in your role model's shoes. Instead of struggling with negotiating with yourself, take your struggles and use your role model's convictions to fight them. Your own internal dialogue is admittedly a little lazy and overly flexible, so what about someone with magnificent self-discipline? What would they do, and how would it differ from your own choice? You instantly know what to do now. You have a new course of action to take that comes from a role model you like and trust.

Above all, having a role model should serve as a reminder that you don't get what you want through inaction.

What if you can't find an accountability partner and there's no role model springing to mind? Well, you can still use that *adult* peer pressure to your favor simply by mentioning your goal or task to someone. It may be someone in your circle of family or friends, or you could post your plans on social media. Make it public, loud, and proud.

Are you going to live up to your proclamations? What will people think? How can you face people after having essentially lied to them? By making your intentions known publicly, you create a sense of accountability.

Of course, here you are being motivated into self-discipline by negative feelings of shame and embarrassment—but remember that it's all about whether you control emotions or you let them control you. While you may have someone call you out on not working toward your goal, this is much more of an internal motivation. There's nothing wrong with being pushed by something negative; the reality is that negativity is a far stronger motivator than anything positive. You would work much harder to avoid being lashed with a whip than you would to eat the fanciest meal in the world.

If you want to lose weight and share it with the world, imagine how you might feel loafing around with your family and friends. Will they say something? Are they thinking about what you said and judging you for eating a family-sized bag of chips? Or even worse yet, did they not take your public proclamation seriously because you're *that* unreliable?

Negative as it may be, it has the real ability to spark action.

By involving others, whether an accountability partner, friend or family member, coach, role model or mentor, or the world of social media, you are held to standards that you might not otherwise keep. Whether you want to explicitly label this as self-discipline is up to you, but if your goal is to get things done, you should use all the tools at your disposal.

Control Your Impulses

One massive step toward improving your self-discipline is to learn to control your impulses. They are polar opposites; one is stable and reliable like a metronome, while the other is unpredictable like a volcano.

An impulse is the sudden need to do (or not do) something, an uncontrollable urge. Impulses are often acted upon without forethought or planning and can come out of nowhere to derail your entire day. This is where self-discipline dies because you are at the mercy of a spur-of-the-moment whim. You can't engage in both at the same time. Control over impulses is a key to consistent discipline.

For instance, imagine that you are playing piano during a big performance, but you get the sudden impulse to scratch an itch on your face. The itch is not urgent, nor is it important, but it's something nagging in the back of your mind that will cause you discomfort unless you address it. Now, will you break your performance to scratch the itch, or will you ignore the temporary distraction? You would probably recognize that your impulse should take a back seat to maintaining self-discipline in this instance.

Only rarely, like the above example, is it clear that we should suppress these random impulses. But just like the piano performance, we don't realize how much indulging in an impulse will throw us off. These things add up, and so does the time required for you to re-focus yourself and get back on the horse of self-discipline.

How can we defeat this type of enemy? First, we must understand it.

Impulses have been the subject of psychological research for many years. Recently, researchers from the European Molecular Biology Laboratory have found strong connections between two parts of the brain related to impulse control: the prefrontal cortex, the part of the brain responsible for complex cognition, personality, decision-making, and social behavior, and the brainstem, the portion of the brain that regulates basic autonomic functions such as heart rate and breathing.

This means that we possess a significant number of connections that allow us to self-regulate and control—it takes a conscious thought in our prefrontal cortex, and it travels to our brainstem for calm and relaxation. When we have a strong link between the two, we can better exercise self-discipline.

However, in the study, scientists found that a condition known as *social defeat* (a negative emotional state) in mice weakened the connection between the prefrontal cortex and the part of the brainstem involved in defensive responses. With a weaker connection, they became more impulsive, wilder, and difficult to calm down. When the researchers used a drug to block the connection between the prefrontal cortex and the brainstem completely, the mice demonstrated even more impulsive behavior.

How does this translate to humans? This research sheds light on what is happening in your brain when you're trying to control an impulse. If we're in an emotional state, the connection between the prefrontal cortex and the brainstem is weakened. We become more impulsive and less self-aware.

We can't very well take drugs to strengthen our neural connections and maintain self-discipline better, but we can try to ensure that our prefrontal cortex is engaged as much as possible. That roughly translates to making decisions based on analysis and rationality versus emotion. Self-discipline won't win in the face of urgency, anxiety, and fear, so you have to let them pass and then keep on keeping on. When we're thinking with our brainstem, which isn't always something we can control, our self-discipline goes out the window.

There are techniques we can implement to help support our desire to better control our impulses. Generally, they involve some sort of delay between feeling the impulse and the reaction you give to it. In other words, the more distance between feeling the itch and scratching the itch, the better. You'll usually find that the impulse simply disappears on its own, which further proves its status as something that is simply masquerading as important (when it's really not).

The power of ten. If you can delay action on your impulses, often you can overcome them. There is something to be said for taking a breath, counting slowly to ten, and giving yourself a moment. Tell yourself to persevere for just ten more seconds when you want to stop, and tell yourself to try something out for just ten seconds when you are delaying starting. That's the power of ten—the mere act of holding yourself back requires self-discipline, and you practice feeling a reaction without acting on it.

The power of ten takes the urgency out of your urge to act immediately. Remember, that's where your brainstem loses its grip over your actions and your prefrontal cortex steps in.

For some impulses, counting to ten won't suffice. For example, if you see something you want to buy but don't really *need*, instead of just taking it to the register to be rung up, you can take ten minutes, the second power of ten. This is the same type of diversionary tactic that neuroscientists have found extremely effective to battle impulse-spending and shopping; just ten minutes drastically reduces the brain's thirsty response for a reward. Rather than rush to purchase the item, you could leave the store for ten minutes, and you'll be less likely to follow through with the purchase.

Usually, an itch will disappear within seconds. A strong emotional spike will mostly dissipate within ten seconds. You might stop seeing red in that time span. Your initial reaction just might have given way to rational thought.

After all, anyone can withstand anything for ten seconds, right? Keep this mantra in mind and bypass the danger zone where your brainstem is in control of your actions.

Label your feelings. A person who doesn't understand his or her emotions is more likely to act on impulse. If you can't identify when you're feeling angry or stressed or embarrassed, you may act in a way that just makes it worse. In essence, if you don't realize what you're feeling, you will be unable to stop it.

For example, suppose you have an argument with someone and you impulsively stomp off and slam the door on your way out. Those behaviors scream anger, but they likely happened so quickly, so impulsively, that you didn't consciously think—you just reacted. By the way, this is precisely the condition under which people later find themselves saying things like, "I'm sorry. I don't know what came over me . . ."

If you took a moment to realize why you want to storm out the door and how angry you are, you would have a better chance of tempering your response. Instead of leaving in a huff, say, "I think I'm feeling angry right now. I should deal with the anger first and then respond after it passes." That takes the acute impulse out of the situation and increases the chance that things will go better once the situation is de-escalated. Basically, it puts a little distance between you and the emotion, so you're not completely swallowed up and identified with it. Labeling your emotions also gives you an exact symptom to deal with—anger, resentment, bitterness, frustration—and from that you can find a roadmap to deal with it. It gives you a verbal "handle" on the feeling so you can talk about it and manage it. That wouldn't be possible without a label.

It's acceptable to feel angry, embarrassed, frustrated, and ashamed. But what *isn't* acceptable is to substitute these initial reactions as your response and act impulsively. When you take a pause to identify what you're feeling, often you will realize that things aren't quite as urgent as you thought. You open up a little space in which your own free will can pause and ask, "What do I want to do here? I am aware of this sensation right now that's pressing me for a reaction, but do I *want* to react to it?"

Write down the facts. Writing down the facts of a situation helps you to clarify what is real, what is not, and what your ideal outcome is. This is related to the power of ten in that you are pausing to sort through the facts before you act impulsively with the brainstem. And of course, you write much more slowly than you think, so this slows your entire reactive process down. That bodes well for the prefrontal cortex and self-discipline.

Thus, when you want to quit something, when you want to delay starting something, or when you suddenly feel an urge to do something unproductive or distracting, write down the facts. Write out what the situation is, what you want to do, and what you should probably do instead. Write down your ideal outcome and how that differs from the path you would take if you gave in to your impulse.

Highlight only what is factual and leave out the rest. Don't write down your feelings, emotions, fears, or anxieties. Keep it black and white. When you have a clear picture of "just the facts, ma'am," you are able to look at the situation objectively and know what you should do. This not only allows you to respond in a more tempered fashion, but it helps you sort out what actually happened versus what you "thought" or "felt" happened.

For example, suppose you had a blow-up with your boss at work, and your impulse is to quit your job and look for a new one. Writing down the facts will help you clarify the situation and sort the emotion from the facts. Maybe the facts are your boss blamed you for a situation; you didn't get to tell your side of the story; you've worked at your current job for eight years; you are the primary breadwinner of your family; in addition to salary, you have good benefits; and you haven't talked to human resources to help resolve the situation. You want to punch his face and quit—that doesn't get you to your ideal outcome. Your ideal outcome involves being heard, being more assertive, and keeping your job.

Suddenly, after taking the time to examine the facts, it's clear what you need to do to maintain self-discipline. An impulse only exists because it is quick and fleeting; under greater scrutiny, they almost all crumble.

Ask "why" five times. A final strategy for helping to control your impulses is asking *why*. This tactic is all about getting to the root of your impulse and hopefully uncovering new information about yourself.

You're actually asking the same or similar question five times in a row, and you'll be surprised to learn that each time, you just might pull out a different answer than before. You're forcing yourself to justify why an impulse should win out over self-discipline. At the end of the process, you'll either be able to answer *why* sufficiently, or you'll come to the conclusion that it was simply an impulse not worth partaking in.

Impulses are never thought through or founded on deep analysis, so you wouldn't expect to be able to answer *why* more than once or twice. Thus, only if you can answer *why* a few times does it pass the sniff test of importance or urgency. Practically speaking, what does this look like? Suppose you have an impulse to break your spending discipline and buy a new sweater.

Why do you want it?
I like it.
Why do you want it?
It's a great price. (This is as far as an impulse will probably carry you.)
Why do you want it?
No real reason other than wanting it . . .
Why do you want it?

Looks cool?
Why do you want it?
I guess I don't, really.

Once you've asked yourself *why* five times in five different ways, you have distilled the main pros and cons for why you should or shouldn't buy the shirt. And really, you've come up with nothing to justify the impulse. If this was really a shirt that you needed in some way, you'd be able to come up with better answers, such as, "Because my other shirt ripped," or, "I have a wedding coming up," or, "I want to look nice for a date!" In those instances, you are *not* dealing with an impulse masquerading as a need—it's an actual need.

Even if it doesn't bring you to the point where you realize you can't answer *why* five times (which is a red flag), at least it will force you to stop and think about your decisions. Whatever the case, you've become more mindful and more likely to be disciplined in your daily life.

Looking at each of these strategies, the common themes involve reflection, self-awareness, and pausing before responding.

Takeaways:

- Self-discipline and habits are innately intertwined. In fact, habits are the natural goal for self-discipline; self-disciplined acts require conscious effort until the point it becomes a natural habit.
- Make it a habit to think about a self-discipline formula, either the one in this book, or one of your own making. It's another way of visualizing exactly what forces are at play regarding your self-discipline. My favorite version: ***Self-discipline = (personal motivation + positive benefits) – (discomfort + distractions).*** Here, if the right side of the equation turns out positive, then you have the pre-requisites for self-discipline. Thus, it becomes a matter of understanding the positive forces (motivation and benefits) and the negative forces (discomfort and distractions) and how they manifest in your life. You may even discover that you are neglecting a few factors, which is just setting yourself up for failure.

- Use the if-then technique to make your decisions before you have to decide to exercise self-discipline. Our worst decisions come when we rely on our strength of character. Thus, plan around them. If X, then Y can be your new best friend, and it is applicable in just about everything we encounter on a daily basis. It turns out we behave better when linked to other things.
- What kind of discipline style should you use, abstinence or moderation? Abstinence provides that there are no exceptions allowed, and it actually gives you a sense of freedom because you won't have to negotiate with yourself on when to start, stop, and feel satisfied. Moderation is when you accept a certain amount of deviation, as long as you can meet your goals and milestones you set out beforehand. There is also freedom here because you can indulge and not feel like you are missing out on anything.
- Peer pressure can be positive. The sad truth is that we are products of our physical and social environments. With regards to the latter, the people around us can sometimes make or break us. Thus, we can construct our social circles

to help us become more self-discipline. You can use accountability partners, role models, mentors, and teachers. You can also dip into the dark side and use the negative emotions of public shame and embarrassment to keep you accountable. After all, we work harder to avoid a punch in the face than to eat our favorite food.

- Impulses are the antithesis of self-discipline. They are unpredictable urges that can *take over* at any point. Studies have shown that impulses are stronger during emotional reactions. Thus, battling impulses is about putting as much time as possible between an emotional reaction and the actual response you give. Delaying tactics, in other words. You can use the ten second/minute rule, label your feelings, write down the facts of a situation without regard to your personal perspective, and ask "why" five times to understand the root of the impulse.

Summary Guide

CHAPTER 1. MIND OVER MATTER

- Self-discipline is the act of putting mind over matter and dictating exactly what your actions and behaviors are. But control over the mind is like saying you want to take a casual stroll to the surface of the sun. It's not easy and must be reined in constantly for you to even have a chance of self-discipline. As it turns out, there are many obstacles to acting disciplined and controlling yourself.
- Buddhism teaches five mental hindrances to self-discipline: giving in to the five senses, animosity and malice, apathy and laziness, anxiety and remorse, and hesitation and doubt. The common thread is that they all require immediate and urgent attention, even if it is fabricated urgency. When you are so focused on the now, the *later* that self-discipline serves becomes wholly unimportant.

- Another aspect of being unable to move past the present moment and plan for the future is how the neurotransmitter dopamine influences our actions. Humans abide by the pleasure principle; we seek pleasure and avoid pain whenever possible, even subconsciously. Acting self-disciplined very rarely brings you pleasure, and most of the time it actively brings some measure of pain or at least discomfort. That's a problem. We must change the way we think about pleasure and pain, and who we want to benefit the most: in most cases, your future self.

- Time orientation is yet another problem with self-discipline. Some of us are present-oriented—this will not serve you well because you won't be able to act in the best interests of future you. Others of us are future-oriented—we think about what we want in the future and work backward to create it. This perspective meshes much better with self-discipline. In the fable of the ant and the grasshopper, the diligent ant is future-oriented and survives the winter, while the hedonistic grasshopper is present-oriented and starves.

- In the end, despite all these obstacles, whether or not you have self-discipline is up to you. This is in a literal sense— the placebo effect has shown that however much you believe you have, that's what you'll have. This is empowering and freeing because it means there is nothing between you and what you want—besides you. It's up to you. This is actually ultimate freedom, not restriction, as self-discipline is sometimes framed. Take it as a challenge to be overcome.

CHAPTER 2. UNDERSTAND THE CYCLE; BREAK THE CYCLE

- It can be tempting to think of your self-discipline as isolated incidents that you must overcome. This would be a mistake. Self-discipline does not exist in a vacuum and is highly dependent on five factors that make up the cycle of self-discipline. Or, more accurately, the cycle of *laziness*.
- The phases are unhelpful assumptions ("Life is short, so I should enjoy it and not spend my precious time washing

that dusty car!"); increasing discomfort from knowingly avoiding responsibility ("I'd rather not wash the car. It's boring and uncomfortable."); excuses to decrease discomfort ("It's perfectly reasonable for me not to wash the car. It's so hot outside I would melt."); avoidance activities to decrease discomfort ("I will clean the bathroom instead. I'm still productive!"); and negative and positive consequences from avoiding responsibility ("Ah, I feel better about myself now. Oh, wait. I still need to wash that car . . .")—at which point you find yourself right back at the beginning, except with less willpower and incentive than before because negative consequences create pessimism, while positive consequences create self-sabotage.

- Aside from knowledge of the cycle and what you tend to fall prey to, there are specific ways to deal with four of the five phases of the cycle. Regarding unhelpful assumptions, instead embody the empowering belief of the forty percent rule. Regarding discomfort, change your expectations and actively practice discomfort to build your mental toughness. Regarding excuses, learn how to reframe your excuses and stop falling into the common traps and self-lies. Regarding avoidance activities, it's a matter of out of sight, out of mind; if you cannot find distractions, you cannot avoid.

- Other general considerations for beating the cycle of lacking self-discipline are creating goals to reduce discomfort and improve time management, and developing skills to stop making excuses so frequently. Beat the cycle!

CHAPTER 3. YES OR NO?

- Yes or no? Just a simple answer, please, with no BS. This chapter is all about self-interrogation and digging into your excuses and rationalizations to avoid exercising self-discipline. What follows is typically self-awareness at how casually you view avoiding work. There are six questions to bring clarity. Most are indeed yes/no questions to force you to either admit a harsh truth or take action.

- Will this course of action create a gap between my ideal self and my non-desired self? Alternatively, does this action take me closer or farther from my goals?
- Does this action truly represent my intentions? If not, then what the heck am I doing?
- Am I merely uncomfortable? Am I letting mere discomfort keep me from my goals? Am I so mentally weak?
- What would I do if I had no choice but to exercise self-discipline? Certainly *not* the worst-case scenario.
- Is "I don't want to" a good enough excuse to not do something? You may have the ability to use this excuse, but what about those who are never able to take a break and *have to act* every single time? It's difficult to feel gratitude and lack self-discipline at the same time.
- Am I doing the *right* thing or the *easy* thing? There's usually only one path to what you want, and it's not typically an easy one.
- Is there a *real* obstacle to my goal that I can't overcome? This focuses you on the fact that most of the time, the so-called obstacle is not the problem, but our

attitude is. If we wanted to do it, no obstacle would stop us, and if we didn't want to do it, we wouldn't, even if there we zero obstacles.

- What is the outcome of this action if I continue along this path? Switch your focus away from instant gratification and see how a decision plays out over time, from ten minutes to ten years into the future. When you choose something, you are also choosing the consequences of that thing, even if those consequences don't kick in for a while.

CHAPTER 4. THE NEUROPSYCHOLOGY OF SELF-DISCIPLINE

- Working with the limitations of your own brain requires an honest appraisal of where you are and how you're functioning. Make it a habit to routinely assess yourself on the following aspects, on a scale of one to ten: Sense of purpose, the presence of positive mentors, sensory rich vision, self-belief, planning and organization, education and skills, patient perseverance, and the ability to see work as play.

- This kind of self-reflection allows you to see exactly what areas you need to work on and see whether your efforts are resulting in progress.
- Depending on which aspects you identify as under-developed, you can do a lot to improve.
- For a stronger sense of purpose, you'll need to work on self-knowledge, and dig deep into your genuine values. To find positive mentors, reach out to others and network, or simply ask for help and advice from accomplished people.
- To develop sensory rich vision, make a goal collage or practice visualization to conjure up a vivid, five-sense image of the end you're aiming for. To increase self-belief, actively court failure and rejection—to prove to yourself that your worth as a person doesn't stem from these things. Meditation, mindfulness, and self-care also go a long way to cultivating self-compassion.
- To have better planning and organization, start by decluttering both your mind and workspace to cut down on distractions. Set up habits that allow you to atomate, delegate and concentrate.

- To build skills and education, keep reading. Become curious, and ask questions, learning where you can. To improve patience and perseverance, focus on the smallest, *sustainable* change you can make and keep up every day. To see work as play, change your language. Don't say, "I have to do XYZ," but instead say, "I choose to do XYZ." Remember, nobody is forcing you to be the best version of yourself.
- Focus on a few main principles for lasting motivation. These include not waiting for a right time, taking baby steps, working from intrinsic motivation, avoid temptation outright, cutting distractions, monitoring impulses with mindfulness, visualizing in detail our goal, getting comfortable with being uncomfortable, and allowing our future selves to advise and guide our present selves.
- Finally, the most important may be to recognize that you will slip up, but will always be ready to forgive, learn from mistakes, and move on to be better next time.

- Self-discipline and habits are innately intertwined. In fact, habits are the natural goal for self-discipline; self-disciplined acts require conscious effort until the point it becomes a natural habit.

- Make it a habit to think about a self-discipline formula, either the one in this book, or one of your own making. It's another way of visualizing exactly what forces are at play regarding your self-discipline. My favorite version: ***Self-discipline = (personal motivation + positive benefits) – (discomfort + distractions).*** Here, if the right side of the equation turns out positive, then you have the pre-requisites for self-discipline. Thus, it becomes a matter of understanding the positive forces (motivation and benefits) and the negative forces (discomfort and distractions) and how they manifest in your life. You may even discover that you are neglecting a few factors, which is just setting yourself up for failure.

- Use the if-then technique to make your decisions before you have to decide to exercise self-discipline. Our worst decisions come when we rely on our strength of character. Thus, plan around them. If X, then Y can be your new best friend, and it is applicable in just about everything we encounter on a daily basis. It turns out we behave better when linked to other things.

- What kind of discipline style should you use, abstinence or moderation? Abstinence provides that there are no exceptions allowed, and it actually gives you a sense of freedom because you won't have to negotiate with yourself on when to start, stop, and feel satisfied. Moderation is when you accept a certain amount of deviation, as long as you can meet your goals and milestones you set out beforehand. There is also freedom here because you can indulge and not feel like you are missing out on anything.

- Peer pressure can be positive. The sad truth is that we are products of our physical and social environments. With regards to the latter, the people around us can sometimes make or break us. Thus, we can construct our social circles to help us become more self-discipline. You can use accountability partners, role models, mentors, and teachers. You can also dip into the dark side and use the negative emotions of public shame and embarrassment to keep you accountable. After all, we work harder to avoid a punch in the face than to eat our favorite food.

- Impulses are the antithesis of self-discipline. They are unpredictable urges that can *take over* at any point. Studies have shown that impulses are stronger during emotional reactions. Thus, battling impulses is about putting as much time as possible between an emotional reaction and the actual response you give. Delaying tactics, in other words. You can use the ten second/minute rule, label your feelings, write down the facts of a situation without regard to your personal perspective, and ask "why" five times to understand the root of the impulse.